DOG People
Do It BETTER

200 Ways Our Dogs Teach Us to Love, Laugh, and Loosen Up

Theresa Mancuso

Adams Media
Avon, Massachusetts

Published by Adams Media, an F+W Publications Company
57 Littlefield Street, Avon, MA 02322 U.S.A.
www.adamsmedia.com

ISBN: 1-59337-206-X

Printed in Canada.

J I H G F E D C B

Library of Congress Cataloging-in-Publication Data
Mancuso, Theresa.
Dog people do it better / by Theresa Mancuso.
p.   cm.
ISBN 1-59337-206-X
1. Dogs—Anecdotes. 2. Dogs—Behavior—Anecdotes.
3. Human-animal relationships—Anecdotes. I. Title.

SF426.2.M35 2004
636.7—dc22

2004009925

This publication is designed to provide accurate and authoritative information with regard to the subject matter covered. It is sold with the understanding that the publisher is not engaged in rendering legal, accounting, or other professional advice. If legal advice or other expert assistance is required, the services of a competent professional person should be sought.
—From a *Declaration of Principles* jointly adopted by a Committee of the American Bar Association and a Committee of Publishers and Associations

Many of the designations used by manufacturers and sellers to distinguish their products are claimed as trademarks. Where those designations appear in this book and Adams Media was aware of a trademark claim, the designations have been printed with initial capital letters.

Interior photography provided by Theresa Mancuso, except for the
photograph on page 212, which was provided by Cindy Tibbits, and the
photograph on page 44, which was provided by Maxine Perchuk.

This book is available at quantity discounts for bulk purchases.
For information, call 1-800-872-5627.

⌂ Contents

⌂ Dedication

DOGS ARE AMONG THE GREATEST unsung heroes of history. This book is dedicated to the memory of dogs that have served humankind throughout the ages, sometimes even laying down their lives, whether in search and rescue; in military service, personal assistance, as guide dogs, hearing dogs, and therapy dogs; or in quietly leading their families out of fiery buildings or saving them in the face of deadly danger.

Let us remember in particular the dogs that served on September 11, 2001, at the site of the World Trade Center disaster in New York City, as well as the heroic dogs that were left behind after military service in Vietnam. This book is also dedicated to police dogs that protect the public safety, especially those that have died in the line of duty.

We must not forget the millions of dogs that live out their days as family pets, making us happy every day. Mutts and purebreds contribute to our lives more than most of us realize. I dedicate this book in a special way to dogs that have suffered at the hands of their humans, abused and betrayed by the people they loved, whether through ignorance or malice.

While dedicated to the dog friends of contributors whose stories are here, this book belongs especially to my own dogs: Grip, Geisty, Cara Mia, Sasha, Natasha, and Abby.

⌂ Acknowledgments

THE WRITERS OF THESE ANECDOTES come from every walk of life. They hail from all over, Canada to Florida, Washington State to the United Kingdom. Young and old, new and experienced, all are dog lovers. To them, my utmost thanks for participating in this unique and wonderful project. Their generosity has made this book possible, and their cooperation has enabled me to do something I always longed to do—to share with others my deep conviction that dogs *really do teach us how to live.*

Special thanks to my good friend and canine colleague, Elli Matlin, for writing the foreword to this book; and to my extraordinary literary agent, Sara Camilli, for her wit, professionalism, and boundless talents; to my project editor at Adams Media, Kate Epstein, almost forty years my junior and many lifetimes my senior in the business of building books.

I appreciate the insights I have gleaned from all of my dog friends and their people, especially, to Mary Shen, my own dogs' "human littermate," who assisted me through the years in raising and training my pack. Thanks to her help, order emerged from the pages of dog stories scattered all over my dining-room table and across the floor to become this book.

A final word of appreciation to the people who continue to encourage me to write, especially my sister Carolina and my niece Cindy, a fellow dog-lover. Thanks to my good friends Esther, Enid, and Maria, who took care of Abby when I most needed them.

Last but not least, thanks to my canine (and feline) kids for making our home a place of love, warmth, and plenty of dog hair and dust! You are with me always, even though your paws on the computer keyboard cause considerable mishap.

⌂ Foreword

I F ANYONE SHOULD WRITE A BOOK about dogs, it's Theresa Mancuso. Her love of animals, good humor, and insight into their personalities is remarkable, and it is always reciprocated by the animals that love her back.

Theresa is my official puppy nail-cutter, puppycuddler, and socializer for all the litters I have had in the fifteen years I have known her. Our dogs have taught us a great deal, both in humility and humanity. If you want to see someone knocked down a peg or two, watch them come out of the obedience ring or off the Schutzhund field after their dog has made a fool of them. While you know that you have only yourself to blame if your dog is not prepared sufficiently, I still believe some dogs do things just to embarrass you, and then sit back and laugh at you while you try to find a patch of grass to crawl under. Yet these same dogs will sacrifice themselves to save us and never hesitate a second in doing so.

By watching our dogs go through serious illnesses, we realize how stoic these wonderful animals are, giving us pause to wonder how we can complain so much about our aches and pains. My mother was a dog breeder, and she used to say that every woman should have to watch a bitch give birth to a litter of puppies before she gave birth to a child. Then there'd be no screaming and carrying on in the delivery room.

Enjoy this anthology about the joys and heartaches of dog ownership, and "May God help us be the people our dogs think we are!"

—Elli Matlin

⌂ Introduction

WHEN ALL THE REST IS TAKEN AWAY and we forget about it, what we remember are the important things, the things that really mattered. Those we have loved and cherished, that which we have worked for, whatever we have pondered in the depths of our hearts, these are the things that will stay with us when we have forgotten all the rest. That's what counts. Every story in this little book is important; every dog and its loving owner has something to tell us. I have included stories that are happy and those that are sad, stories about working dogs and stories about beloved pets. I wrote this book to give a voice to everyone who wanted to participate, for each one is an important part of the whole.

Dogs teach us a great deal about the art of living, but only if we are willing to learn. As the wise man said, "Only he who is wise and considers them diligently" will benefit by these stories. Many people don't consider dogs or other animals a very important part of life. They hardly give them a second thought, even if they live with them. Some unfortunate individuals even look upon dogs as mere commodities to be sold or transferred as whim dictates, objects of profit and convenience. Others see dogs as tools for work, their labors counting as nothing more than extensions of the handler for his own ends and to his own credit.

But *some* know dogs to be the gifts of heaven that they truly are, furry angels walking beside us, before us, and behind us, surrounding us with the powerful energy of their love and loyalty, life-giving spirits. Dogs are a special manifestation of

the Creator's goodness and generosity. Dressed in fur, they are forever fashionable to the heart. Barking, they contribute to the medley of sound that is the symphony of time and space, the music of everything that is. Far more incorruptible than we are, dogs have a lot to teach us, if only we would pay attention.

These dog stories are brief lessons in living, given to us in the simplest and most direct language. As we do, so shall we become. Dogs know not pride, arrogance, or deceit. They are humble in their truth, and their message goes forth in everything they do. It is all about what matters, the important things that last. You might think your dog is hardly such as this at all. Take another look, please. Pay attention.

As I compiled these anecdotes, I visualized the dogs and people in every story. I sensed their circumstances and felt the flow of their mutual affection. I touched them for a moment and enjoyed the sweet caress of a doggie paw upon my knee, the sound of barks and whistles, the antics of canine kids in eternal quest for dog-fun, human acceptance, understanding, love—and a meaty bone.

When I grow too old to walk my dog, too blind to see its beauty, too feeble to reach out and hug its furry shoulders or press its rugged head against my chest, when I grow too old to love my canine companion and cherish it for its deep devotion, too self-occupied to pay attention to its teaching me how to live, then it shall be time for me to cross the rainbow bridge where my departed canine friends from the past await me. In their company, I shall be whole again and glad.

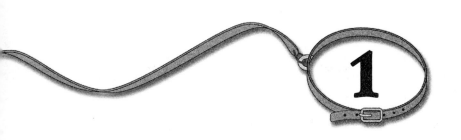

Puppy Love:
Romance and Friendship

T HE THINGS THAT MEAN MOST in our lives are illuminated by the things we have loved most and cherished best. The bonds of love and friendship that we form with others give us strength and power to endure through all the days of our lives. Friendship and romantic love are powerful motivating forces. They touch us at our deepest level of our being and sculpt our lives for better or for worse.

Among life's truest friends are the canine companions we have known along the way. They have blended their very essences with our own, and we are blessed for having known their unconditional love. The ability to love unconditionally is not often found in human beings. But when we do strive for it, with generosity of spirit and tenderness of heart, and when we are motivated by diligent compassion and strengthened by inner resolve, then sometimes we are given the great and awesome gift of reciprocity in unconditional love.

From the following anecdotes, we can glean a little bit about unconditional love and abiding friendship, loyalty, devotion, forgiveness, and endurance. Dogs amaze us with their ability to go the whole distance for those they love. I'd like to be exactly like my dog. Wouldn't you?

🏠 Who Do You Love?

by Mary Frenzel-Berra

TUMI WAS DUMB AND PECULIAR, TOO. Our other dogs picked up on that right away. She couldn't find her way out of a corner. She'd fall asleep with her head and front paws on the couch and her rear legs on the floor. When the doorbell rang, our other dogs raced straight to the front door while Tumi went to all the wrong doors to wait for our guests. We'd have to go get her and bring her out front to meet people. She adored it and was always delighted to see guests.

After her replacement surgery for an injury, Tumi would raise her good leg to show us the boo-boo as if she didn't know which leg had been hurt. She often seemed to forget who we were, and we'd have to get acquainted all over again.

But Tumi did one thing perfectly. Ask her, "Tumi, who do you love?" and wait a minute for cognition to strike, and she'd respond to us excitedly and right on the money, wagging her tail enthusiastically. She also responded to her patients in the rehab center and to kittens, obedience judges, turtles, and other living things. When she was euthanized in 1999, I claimed I'd never want to have another stupid dog. But as time went on, I missed Tumi enormously. Who do you love?

∞ *In the final analysis, it's all about love. Brains are nice, and looks are great, but love is all you need.*

⌂ A Rude Awakening

by Dr. Nancy Bekaert

W E ALL LIKE TO BANDY THE PHRASE "ALPHA DOG" around, but I discovered that with that title comes an awesome responsibility. I now realize that although I may be the alpha member of my pack, I will never be an "alpha dog."

One winter day on the beach at Coney Island, my four dogs and I were confronted by a pack of feral dogs. Ten or fifteen dogs charged out from under the boardwalk and began to fan out as they approached us. With my back to the ocean, they had cut off my escape. For the first time in twenty-five years of teaching (and preaching) about dog behavior, I was suddenly up close and personal with the awesome workings of the pack mentality. As they closed in, I had no choice but to send my own pack out to what I feared might be their deaths.

My alpha shepherd (a true alpha in every sense of the word) headed straight for the pack leader. With about fifty feet left between them, the two packs stopped. The two alpha dogs approached each other. With hackles up, they circled and postured. In less than a minute, the feral dog lowered his head, turned, and led his pack back under the boardwalk. My shepherd trotted back to me. As I clung to his neck hugging and kissing him, he looked at me as if to say, "What's all the fuss? It's all in a day's work for an alpha dog."

∞ *The loyalty and courage of the alpha dog is legendary. Ours pales by comparison. We, too, must learn loyalty and the courage to take our rightful place with those who depend on us.*

🏠 Funny Dog

by Louise Maguire

M Y BRIDGET HAS AN OFFBEAT SENSE OF HUMOR. At dawn she sits squarely on top of me, licking. There's no point in my sliding under the covers because a nimble paw will rake them ruthlessly away. Polite kisses swiftly become slurps and nibbles. I admit defeat and make the prewalk coffee. Meanwhile, Bridget is curled up and cozy, her pretty head on my pillow and one puppy tooth showing. I have to smile.

She likes to supervise my toilet arrangements, biting the cold inflow, or drinking some flavorsome dirty bathwater. Bridget drops selected toys on my unprotected feet, or throws them into the bath or down the toilet. She snatches away the bathmat, sponge, and even soap, or tickles my bare flesh unmercifully with her long tongue until I am forced to giggle with delight.

Phone calls are boring to Bridget, so she thrusts her rope at me and growls ferociously. While I work at the computer, she stands beside me and nudges my fingers. Glancing out the window, she barks unexpectedly and when I rise to look, she immediately steals my vacated chair. Hilariously nonsensical messages appear onscreen, Bridget's work.

She scrubs her supple back on carpets, legs ridiculously twisted and wipes her face on cushions, groaning with pleasure. She rolls and squirms in ecstasy, grinning. And why do I laugh so much with her? Because I remember the rescued, stressed, and repressed Bridget of one year past.

∞ Nothing is so healing as a loving home in which heart and mind can recover from the traumas of life as the body grows strong again.

....

⌂ A Canine Queen

by Stephanie Nolasco

IFI HAS BEEN MY COMPANION SINCE I was very young. I cannot tell you at what age I first laid eyes on the "queen," not without getting emotional. Yes, she's antique, but she's fully immortal in my eyes. Fifi has seen everything that I've experienced in my lifetime, yet as I grew up, she never dared to comment on any of my wild decisions. Now she simply lies in her cozy bed, watching a loud Dominican household argue about everything imaginable. She accompanies my mother watching soap operas and makes sure to scare away all my lurid dreams with her boisterous snores. Whenever a rap or knock sounds at the door, Fifi morphs into an untamed lion and growls her lungs out, exposing the razor-sharp pearls of her teeth. She's not just the housedog, she's a member of our family that provides love to all and guards us from harm.

Yet she never misses an opportunity to have her back scratched or to enjoy a delicious Hispanic meal. Fifi is bilingual and responds to both English and Spanish. How many dogs can do that? My only regret is that she never had a chance to create an heir to her throne.

Truly my queen, Fifi will live on forever in my heart as the goddess she portrays herself to be.

∞ *In love and friendship, fidelity and constancy are paramount. The memory of true devotion is eternal ballast for the soul because genuine love and friendship are fundamental to well being.*

· · · · · · · · · · · · · ·

 ## Korki

by Roni Henning

WHEN I LEARNED that Korki was going into a shelter, I agreed to find him a home. A strange-looking collie, his big head and long nose overshadowed his tiny eyes. He was eleven months old, and with three failed adoptions, I was the last-chance hotel. My husband, John, was sitting comfortably on the sofa the day Korki arrived. He bypassed me to lay his head in John's lap. Excessive crating had made Korki aggressive. He lunged and snarled at people and dogs alike. I refused to walk him, so John got the job. He loved it, returning from their walks telling me how good Korki was. "You lie," I said, but John just laughed.

Our small apartment barely housed three bunnies and one collie, let alone two! I sought potential adopters everywhere. John, however, was bonding. Another dog owner confided, "Your husband says, 'My wife thinks I'm looking for a home for

Korki, but I'm not. I'm keeping him.'" When I confronted John with a childish, "The dog's going or I'm going," he said, "Korki stays; I love him." So Korki and I started obedience classes.

One week before Korki graduated, John died suddenly of a heart attack. In a few minutes, my life was altered forever. Gradually, I came to feel John's presence in Korki. Eleven years passed, and before my eyes, my beautiful Korki became old and arthritic. When the pain intensified so he couldn't walk, I had him put to sleep, the hardest thing I ever did. Now, John is walking him once more.

∞ *Loss and separation are inevitable, for nothing is forever. Learning to accept one's fate and make peace with one's destiny is the Mt. Everest we must climb in the spiritual life.*

⌂ "Am I My Brother's Keeper?"

by Elli Matlin

I HAVE SEVERAL OLD DOGS that have been companions for a long time. Two of them, Genny and Cairo, have lived together for about seven years, ever since I got Genny back for the third time and decided that she was destined to remain here with me. I never realized just how strong a bond these two dogs had until one recent night. Genny suffers from canine vestibular syndrome, which makes her unsteady on her feet and causes her to hold her head tilted to one side. Accidentally, she became impaled on the metal hook that holds the water bucket in her crate. The hook pierced the skin near her eyebrow—fortunately, it did not damage her eye. Genny was pinned, but she never said a word. Cairo, however, raised such a ruckus that I was awakened from a sound sleep. I rushed in to see why he was carrying on, only to find Genny with the bucket attached to her head.

I opened the crate door and gently pushed Genny closer to the pail at one side of her crate so that I could remove the hook from her eyebrow. It was a very delicate maneuver, but everything went fine. As soon as Genny was successfully released, Cairo settled down peacefully and did not make another peep. "Am I my brother's keeper?" Obviously, Cairo thinks so!

∞ *We are all connected all the time. We are all responsible for the welfare and happiness of one another and the preservation of the earth.*
....

⌂ Hey, Mom! Now, Mom?

by Theresa Mancuso

D O DOGS UNDERSTAND WHAT WE SAY? It appears that Cara Mia did! When my male German shepherd, Grip, was ten months old, my female, Cara Mia, came into heat. I did not want to breed them at such a young age, and rather than allow Grip to be tormented by the appealing aroma of a female in heat, I decided to board Grip until Cara Mia's breeding days had passed. She missed him dreadfully, for they had been inseparable buddies.

The night before Grip's scheduled pickup at the boarding kennel, I told Cara Mia not to worry. "We're getting Grippi tomorrow," I repeated several times that day and throughout the evening. Each time I said it, Cara Mia gave me an anticipatory doggie smile, her eyes sparkling with eagerness. Then she did something she had never done before and has never done since! She awakened me every few hours during the night, nudging at my pillow, licking my face and putting a paw on my bed, pleading, it seemed, for dawn to come. Her eyes spoke volumes.

The next morning, I rose and dressed hurriedly with an insistent German shepherd pushing me along. As we departed for the boarding kennel, there was no doubt in my mind that Cara Mia understood exactly what was happening. We drove to Connecticut, and when the dogs saw each other, Grip and Cara Mia's joy knew no bounds. Home together at last!

∞ *Separation from loved ones is a difficult and inevitable fact of life, sweetened only by the happiness of reuniting. In the absence of physical presence, memory serves to keep love alive and growing until we meet again.*

 Dog Pals

by Louise Maguire

M Y CROSSBREED BRIDGET'S A BORN COMEDIAN, running rings around canine accomplices. She's smart, quick, sneaky, and full of surprises. She adores the chase, preferably brandishing someone else's trophy.

Veteran Irish setter Ria's an easy target. Ria drops her squeaky toy to permit sniffing, nose to nose, then pirouettes to allow for delicate investigation under her feathery tail. Bridget ignores canine etiquette. She grabs Ria's toy and accelerates out of reach.

Jodie the golden retriever shares Bridget's passion for sticks. Jodie's current branch permits a noisy tug of war. The branch finally breaks, and two contented winners each brandish half—until Jodie unwisely takes a breather. Bridget snaffles both pieces of branch and shoots away, prancing with joy.

Sugar is a laid-back golden retriever with no competitive ambition. When Bridget steals Sugar's rubber ring, she just turns over to display her abundant underwear, apparently laughing.

Labrador Jess likes to display her trophies. Bridget circles the innocent retriever and snaps off most of the stick that Jess is proudly carrying. Jess's confused puppy face is unforgettable as Bridget tangos away with the spoils.

Bridget shows miniature schnauzer Katy how to hunt for mice in long grass. She suddenly leaps out brandishing a lost rubber bone, with Katy in desperate pursuit. Our laughter acknowledges Bridget's victory circuit.

The action slows down a bit as toy poodle Candy appears. She was a minute runt with a deformed leg and remains a ridiculous fluffy ball of fluff too frail for adult games. Bridget is always gentle with her. No contest here. Candy rules, okay?

∞ *Every friend is unique and special, to be appreciated and loved as an individual. Treat each of your friends as if he or she were the only person in all of the world.*

⌂ The Dog I Didn't Want

by Dr. Sue Ann Lesser

THERE WAS A DOG THAT HAD BEEN RESCUED from a snowstorm by one of the exercise riders at Aqueduct racetrack. Cindy was a mixture of corgi, perhaps, with its huge satellite dish ears, and basset with speckling and ticking and that type of body shape plus a hint of bandy legs. Who knows what else she was? My fiancé was the foreman in the racing stable where Cindy came to live. She rapidly became a favorite of Michael's because she was a serious chicken killer. Chickens excrete their bodily wastes all over the hay that the horses must eat, and chicken dung is hazardous to horses already stressed from the rigors of racing. There are lots of chickens at Aqueduct because many of the stable hands, unfortunately, raise them for fighting.

One such stable hand took huge exception to Cindy's

attacks on his fighting cocks and threatened to run her through with a pitchfork. Michael stopped him, and that evening asked me if Cindy could come home with him "on trial." I acquiesced although I really didn't want another dog. Our Dobie mix, P-Nutty, another adoption from the stable, was such a handful. Besides, I hated the name Cindy.

I renamed her Bandy after the look of her legs. When Bandy ate one of the couch cushions, it became apparent that she was not trustworthy to be left at home alone, so Bandy came with me in my vet mobile to the track and on all my other calls.

She rapidly became my trusted and faithful companion and the most wonderful dog I've ever owned. The dog I didn't want became my best friend.

∞ *Sometimes, the one we least expect to be our friend turns out to be the closest friend of all, the dearest and the best. Life is full of surprises, and we never know what's around the next corner.*

🏠 Always Stay on Your Toes!

by Terri J. Stafford

GARY AND I LIVE IN A SMALL, RURAL COMMUNITY in Maine with our six dogs, most of them rescued from terrible situations. One day as I was feeding the gang, chaos erupted. Bumper, a three-year-old bullmastiff/American bulldog mix, is a big, goofy guy, too smart for his own good. He tried to weasel his way into Wheezy's spot. She growled at him ferociously, so Bumper tried to grab her.

"Enough," I hollered, and the big guy let go. Just then, Hilda, a ten-year-old pit bull/shepherd/Husky mix, joined by Razzmatassus, a one-year-old bullmastiff, came crashing into the living room to join in the fray. I put Bumper, the trouble-maker, into my bedroom as Kalli ran into the kitchen to rumble with Wheezy. Sage, an eleven-year-old pit, grabbed hold of Kalli, but let go when I corrected her. I got Sage into her crate and Razztus into his. Alone in the house, I knew I had to lock up the dogs safely before I could do anything for poor Wheezy, who finally rested in my lap until Gary came home and found us there.

The entire episode erupted quickly and lasted about eight minutes, but it felt like eight hours.

∞ *Arguments can erupt out of nowhere. Sometimes they can even destroy relationships and friendships when hurtful words and actions bite too deeply to endure. You don't always have a chance to stop and think, so learn in advance how to govern your tongue and mind your behavior to avoid saying or doing something you'll regret when the heat's on. Be prepared for misunderstandings that are just a fact of life. Deal kindly, and nip all forms of jealousy in the bud.*

⌂ Shifting Power, Stable Priorities

by Maxine Perchuk

WHEN I FIRST BROUGHT WILHELMINIA HOME from the shelter, she was a tiny white four-pound fluff ball, gentle and sweet. Beatrice, my basset hound, immediately put her in her place by snapping her away from the food bowl, a demonstration of power in the pack. The entire first year, fifty-pound Bea ate her own dinner, then regularly licked up the remains of twenty-pound Wilhelminia's food bowl, maintaining her alpha position. The following year, a kind of equality began to emerge as both dogs, immediately after eating their own dinners, went to each other's bowls to scavenge and lick the bowls clean.

At some point, the balance of power shifted dramatically, and a new alpha stepped forth. Willie claimed Bea's bowl in the kitchen and banished Bea to her former bowl in the bedroom. Now, Willie taunts Bea by refusing to eat her own dinner for several hours, during which time Bea sits at the kitchen threshold crying and plotting how she will abscond with the uneaten food. Willie is aware of Bea's intentions. Periodically she growls at Bea to keep her at bay. In response, Bea looks upward, as if she were a tourist checking street signs.

"Me? Are you talking to me?"

Ultimately, Willie will allow Bea back into the room, but the moment Willie gets preoccupied, Beatrice will pounce on the remaining food, proving, I suppose, that although a basset will relinquish her alpha status, dinner is an altogether different matter.

⚭ Position and power ebb and flow in life. The same holds true in relationships. Compromise is the way of peace among people. Often, we must give a little to get a lot.

···

⌂ Changing the Chain of Command

by Dottie Seuter

K ELLY, MY GERMAN SHEPHERD, could have been warden at a maximum-security prison. She knew all the rules and strictly enforced them with the others in our pack. God help Degen or Anja if they ever touched something that Kelly knew was forbidden property, or if they tried to scoot out the door ahead of me. Heaven forbid the younger dogs should walk in my flowerbeds or do any other naughty act. Pack matron Kelly, super warden, would quickly and firmly discipline them in whatever way she deemed appropriate for the offense. The younger dogs never challenged her authority. They simply accepted that Kelly was in charge.

A month before she died, at age thirteen, we were all out in the yard when suddenly, without warning and for no reason, Anja, the second female, attacked Kelly right in front of me. Kelly went down immediately, but Anja continued the assault. Degen would have joined in, but when I gave him a platz (down) command, he obeyed and remained where he was. I had to use a shovel to get Anja to stop her aggression against Kelly before she killed her.

The power structure was irrevocably changed. Anja took over, and Kelly accepted it. It was much harder for me to deal with it than for Kelly. She knew it was just the way things were; she couldn't command Anja any longer. I understood that, too, but I also knew in my heart that what had occurred was a sign that we didn't have much time left together. Unfortunately, I was correct.

∞ *The wisdom of a peaceful heart comes from accepting the great truth that everything changes and nothing is forever, not even the security of a great love. Be prepared to let go when it's time, and you'll always be free.*

⌂ Bear's Rescue

by Bob Osgoodby

BEAR, MY EIGHT-MONTH-OLD golden retriever puppy, wandered onto the ice on the Shrewsbury River and fell through it. He was immersed in approximately thirty-degree water for over an hour, and we had no way to get to him. While we watched, he vainly tried to climb back up on the ice but could not. Anyone who has a pet can understand the anguish I felt.

My neighbor called the police. The marine police boat was snowed in, so the officers borrowed one from the owner of the Cove Marina. Then Sea Bright Patrolman Brett Friedman and State Trooper Gerard Gallo went out on the ice, dragging the boat behind them for safety and wearing dry suits.

State Trooper Gallo lay flat on the ice trying to get Bear, but the ice gave way, and he also fell into the water. He was able to grab Bear and hand him up to Officer Friedman, who then pulled Trooper Gallo from the water. They brought the dog back to the shore. There's no way I can adequately thank the people who participated in Bear's rescue.

The encouraging postscript to this story is that Sea Bright Police Chief William Moore immediately went out and purchased rescue equipment to deal with falls into the ice. While Bear was able to survive the rigors of the exposure, a child might not have been so lucky. Thanks to my lucky pup, such prolonged immersion in icy water will never happen in my town again.

∞ *Teamwork, combined with bravery and determination, can turn tragedy into victory.*

 The Devoted Couple

by Elli Matlin

ABOUT TWELVE YEARS AGO, there lived across the street an old lady with two dogs that followed her every day when she went garbage-picking around the neighborhood. When her relatives realized that she was unable to care for herself, they placed her in a nursing home, and the two dogs were left homeless on the street. My neighbors and I fed them until we learned that someone had notified animal control to pick them up. Before the dogcatchers could get there, I called the two dogs into my yard and locked the front gate.

Dad and I named them Mr. and Mrs., and a proper couple they were. Mrs. was a friendly Chow mix, and Mr. looked to be part shepherd, but he was shy and fearful. Mr. was completely dependent on Mrs. We knew from the beginning that if anything should happen to Mrs., Mr. could not survive on his own.

They refused to come into the house, so I purchased two doghouses and placed them on the covered front porch, rotating them every season to face the best direction according to weather conditions. Both doghouses were insulated and I kept them furnished with blankets, comforters, and pillows for added comfort. For ten years, they were ideal tenants and lived happily in my front yard, a comfortable and proper estate for such a devoted couple.

∞ *Where charity and love prevail, there's always room for one more. Even the animals remind us that love is a most precious bond to be cherished and preserved at all cost.*

⌂ Don't Judge a Dog by Its Looks

by Yvette Piantadosi-Ward

I LEARNED ONE OF LIFE'S MOST important lessons from my ugliest canine female, a dog called Chubby. She taught me to look past the exterior of an animal in order to see into its heart and soul. Chubby, bless her heart, was by far the homeliest dog

I have ever had the privilege to own, but she was also the smartest and most adaptive, as well as being the world's best mom. Her qualities left a lasting legacy.

Chubby consistently produced beautiful and intelligent puppies. Her nurturing instinct was unequalled. She even stole puppies from other canine mothers and took care of them herself, teaching them appropriate dog behavior such as she taught her own canine babies. The other dogs in our household always respected Chubby and deferred to her.

Chubby had a superb "can do" attitude about everything. She loved to please. She did whatever I asked of her to perfection and seemed to love carrying out my commands. My ugly duckling taught me to look past physical characteristics and see the gem that often lies behind a rough exterior. How I wish I had a dozen more just like Chubby!

ↂ Look beyond appearances to see what lies within. Cherish the spiritual qualities of people for they are greater than power, prestige, or good looks.
....

⌂ Maximus, Farewell

by Theresa Mancuso

NOTHING LASTS FOREVER, not even Maximus, my four-pound Siamese powerhouse. Never have I seen such a tiny kitten with such a loud voice. Max came from a backyard breeder who was about to drown her for being undersized. It was Max's good fortune to miss the bucket by seconds and find for herself, instead, a German shepherd household where she was destined to raise two cats and four pups. Not bad for a runt.

Max educated each new puppy as it came into our home and enforced the rules for our peaceable kingdom, where she was queen. Swatting everyone who transgressed, Max maintained control of even the most recalcitrant canines, and they adored her.

When my dog Grip stole a turkey drumstick one gusty Thanksgiving day, Max followed him fearlessly around the house until he plopped down to devour his booty. She crouched beside him and managed to get her spoils as well. But eventually, the engine of that little body wore down. On Memorial Day, 2000, our eighteen-year-old Max, worn out from her labors of love, died quietly at home, surrounded by her canine kids, three large German shepherds she had raised from infancy. Together with Nikki, her Tonkinese companion, and the dogs Maxi loved.

∞ *Genuine authority comes from within, independent of size or stature.*
················

🏠 Bridget and Her Boyfriends

by Louise Maguire

B RIDGET HAS PLENTY OF BOYS in her life. Hamish, a smart West Highland white, races for the park hoping Bridget will be waiting, nose high, willing unwary squirrels to join the chasing games. Hamish likes to clamber on top of any dog that's lying down. Obligingly, Bridget throws herself down, but she springs up again before Hamish can pile aboard. When Hamish is bribed away, Bridget skims under his nose, swiping his biscuit.

Tiger is a typical boxer, fit, muscular, always ready to gallop. He runs shoulder-to-shoulder with Bridget, sideswiping her. They rear up, front paws batting like playful colts. Her stamina outlasts his snorting efforts, and they relax.

Wise old mongrel Corrie's tooth clamps his ball as Bridget stalks him. He pauses for serious tree checking and marking. Stealthily, she glides in. She slides out delicately, holding her bootie, then parades before him, tail arched, eyes dancing. Corrie's determined pursuit fails miserably.

Max, the rescued Staffordshire terrier cross, once condemned as untrained, dirty, and aggressive, wears the biggest smile in the park today. He never lets Bridget pinch his ball, though he enjoys a slow-motion wrestling match. Max tries to subdue Bridget with his weight. She squirms away and pretends to choke him to death. He loves it.

Storm the German shepherd is Bridget's favorite boy, and she becomes very jealous when he courts another bitch instead. Only she is allowed to be fickle.

∞ *Never surrender being yourself for the pleasure of being popular.*

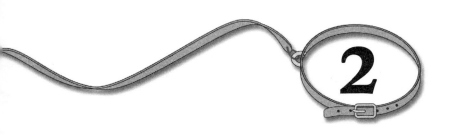

Littermates:
Virtues for Family Living

HUMANS ARE GREGARIOUS ANIMALS. We tend to live in packs, just like dogs, creating families, partnerships, and communities. In dog life, the hierarchy of the pack gets established early on. Members of the pack tend to accept the alpha male and alpha female, taking their own places in the ranks. In family life, the microcosm of human society, peace and happiness depend on establishing order with authority firmly accepted and fairly exercised. To live in peace within our families, we must see our parents and siblings as the individuals that they are. We must accept them with their virtues and their flaws, realizing that we, too, have ours.

In a litter of puppies, siblings depend at first upon their mother. Gradually, their dependence shifts to each other for play and companionship. Ultimately, they go forth from the nest to new families of their own, where once again they must take their place in the hierarchy of the home. Dogs are tolerant of reality, and usually they're completely in tune with it. They do not balk or kick against the goad. They measure up by taking life as it is. Wherever you find yourself in the pack that you're in, whether it's family, community, or relationship with friends, cultivate the virtues of family living. You'll find true happiness in the midst of all the challenges of living and working together.

🏠 Preparing for Parenthood

by Audrey Elias

W HEN I GOT MY GERMAN SHEPHERD, Jenna, I was single and in my late twenties. I used to joke that Jenna was practice for raising children. I had no idea how absolutely right I was until I had my family!

As you go about housebreaking a puppy, you have to develop a certain toughness about—ahem—various unpleasant bodily products. The luxury of excusing yourself from the room when there's vomit to be cleaned up is no longer yours.

You have to be consistent in your behavior and expectations because both dogs and kids are inclined to try to get away with whatever they can. They are happiest if they know exactly what's expected of them, what will happen if they're good, and what will happen if they're disobedient.

Jenna tested me periodically throughout her life. "Does heel still mean that I have to walk right next to you? When you say, 'Sit,' do you still expect me to do it right away?" Kids do exactly the same.

Jenna wasn't perfect. She could take your whole hand in her mouth and would pull you along to let you know she was happy to see you. Jenna also loved to charge straight up to other dogs and greet them with a loud bark. You must learn to let go and accept that a dog—or child—has lovable traits and shortcomings, too.

∞ *Dogs are here to help us learn how to parent children,*
whether they're our own kids, or any of the many other little
folks who come into our lives throughout the duration.

🏠 Big Brother Is Watching

by Kathy Hayden

I LOVE HAVING FOUR GERMAN SHEPHERDS. They're always doing something funny or endearing. One of my favorite memories is of my young male, when I brought him to view his mother's new litter of puppies. As she lay in her whelping box, he jumped up on my bed, put his paws on the footboard, and watched the puppies from his perch. His curious and excited expression as he viewed our new additions was priceless to behold, and it was very clear to all of us observing that he couldn't wait to play with them.

At last, when the pups were five weeks old, he was allowed to join them in their yard. He plopped down, belly up, and let the puppies climb all over him. As they bit him and tugged at his tail, he just smiled, a perfect big brother.

We kept one of those pups for ourselves, and today the brothers are the best of friends.

∞ *Family life thrives when siblings love and care for one another. When brothers and sisters accept one another for who they are, the bond of blood is thicker than any other.*

🏠 Moose and the Telephone Wire

by Claudette Schafer

W E BOUGHT THIS ALASKAN MALAMUTE puppy in January, 2003, to add a new bloodline to our kennel. When I first saw him and the size of his paws, I wanted to name him Big Foot, but my husband thought he'd have a personality complex, so we called him Moose instead.

As Moose was growing up, he learned how to play tug-of-war. When he had no littermates to play with, we'd take a rope and tie it to a tree and Moose would pull and pull.

When Moose was eleven months old, he weighed in at 143 pounds. One day my husband decided to repair the telephone line in the master bedroom and save us the cost of a repair bill. At some point in the process, Harry left the area for a few minutes. When he came back, Moose had ripped out the telephone line totally. Moose probably recognized the line's similarity to the rope tied on the tree outdoors and decided to play a little tug-of-war. My husband took the phone line away from him and threw it into the garbage. In the meantime, Moose saw more line hanging from the telephone box. He not only pulled out the rest of the line but the telephone box as well.

The cost of the telephone repair that my husband was trying so hard to avoid was doubled as the end result of Moose's activities.

∞ *Be careful what you teach kids and pups.*

⌂ Doting Dad

by Theresa Mancuso

AMONG GRIP'S MANY REMARKABLE VIRTUES was his staunch devotion to Geisty, his only daughter. Grip sired a single litter of four sons and a daughter. The day I brought Geisty home, I presented her to Grip, saying, "Here's your baby, Grip." He licked the new pup from head to toe. She climbed up on his shoulders—he was lying on his favorite mat—and commenced to chew on his jowls with unrelenting enthusiasm, her baby paws locked around his blocky head as far as she could stretch. Grip always let Geisty do whatever she pleased. He doted on her.

Grip loved Geisty enormously. They played together constantly along with Cara Mia, my other German shepherd female. The three of them found ways to communicate about everything, and Geisty was the center of attention. If I scolded Grip or Cara Mia, Geisty would run to comfort the older dog, licking his or her face compassionately. Like my own dad and me, Geisty loved a good joke, and so did her father.

When Geisty became a mom several years later, she whelped seven strong and healthy puppies. Whenever Grip walked among his infant grandchildren, he carefully lifted his thick-boned legs and huge, cat-like paws to avoid stepping on the kids. Axios, Geisty's firstborn son, was remarkably determined to hang out with Grandpa Grip. From a young age, Axios scaled the barrier of the puppy room (my kitchen) and scurried off to take his place beside Grandpa Grip on their favorite mat in the living room. My aged father loved to watch Grip with his family and dubbed him "The Loving Grandfather."

> ∞ *Every generation gives birth to the next, and the thread of life continues, carrying on the strongest genetic endowments of the past. Let each generation appreciate those that went before and those that will come after.*

....

⌂ A Tale of Three Diggers

by Elli Matlin

GENNY OF HIGHLAND HILLS was the pick bitch of a litter we had several years ago. Genny was sold at eight weeks to what we thought would be a great home. It turned out not to be so. Locked outdoors in a pen by herself, Genny had little or no socialization until I got her back at over two years of age. She didn't know how to interact with other dogs. Instead, she had learned to entertain herself by digging trenches in the yard. Genny would dig not just downwards, but under the dirt horizontally as well—as we thought, in her attempt to make an escape tunnel.

When I got Genny back and bred her, we kept her daughter, Ruppette, who learned to dig with Genny. When Ruppette's brother, Quite a Guy, was used at stud, I got a puppy back that I named Highland Hills Sally Ann. Now, Sally Ann has also learned to follow Grandma Genny in the digging of holes.

At this point, we have a community dig fest when the three dogs go out together. Ruppette and Sally Ann are not quite as enthusiastic diggers as Grandma Genny, but they hold their own. All three diggers were very surprised one day when one of Genny's tunnels collapsed on them in the rainy season. I have never seen such muddy dogs in all of my life.

∞ *Remember your roots no matter where life takes you. And remember since you and your siblings share a common heritage, what annoys you in your brother or your sister might well be one of your own characteristics, too.*

⌂ The Dog Who Raised a Kitten

by Theresa Mancuso

M Y GERMAN SHEPHERD PUPPIES were always nurtured by my cats, Max and Nikki. The cats would swat at the dogs when they behaved inappropriately according to feline standards. Abby was the last pup to be raised by Max and Nikki, but she never forgot the debt she owed the feline species. When Max died, I purchased Primo, a British shorthair, to be Nikki's companion. Instead, Abby immediately partnered up with my Primo, and the two drove Nikki crazy with kitten-and-dog antics. When Nikki expired at eighteen, I adopted a red tabby from the shelter. Marmaduke Rodgers, a veritable feline gangster, was the complete opposite of my feline gentleman Brit, Primo.

From day one, Abby considered the tiny red kitten her child. She covered Marmaduke's entire body with her large mouth, jaws resting tenderly around his head, shoulders, and tummy while his tiny paws caressed her face. Abby licked him from head to toe like a newborn pup. Wherever Abby went, Marmaduke followed. They cuddled together from the beginning. Primo watched from afar: "You mean *he's* actually here to stay?" It was soon apparent that although I had obtained Marmaduke to be Primo's companion, Marmaduke adores Abby. Marmaduke constantly plays mischievous tricks on Primo, but alas, whenever he starts trouble, Abby rushes in to protect her "baby" from Primo's disciplinary attempts. Indeed, Abby and Marmaduke are a mother-and-son team, of two species but one heart.

∞ *Mother love is a quality that defies the odds. Mothers willingly risk everything to protect and nurture their young. What we owe our mothers is beyond recompense.*

🏠 A Coming Out Party

by Neal C. Jennings

DEETTE AND HER GOLDEN RETRIEVER, Teddy, were asked to visit a special lady at the Meridian Point Rehabilitation Hospital in Scottsdale, Arizona. Teddy, a champion and holder of obedience titles, was a seasoned therapy dog with Pets on Wheels of Scottsdale. The lady had refused to leave her room during her three-week stay, and for good reason: She had lost her sight as the result of a horrible attack. She was suffering, both physically and psychologically. She could no longer see, and she was still in great pain from the attack.

Teddy's task was to get the lady to make those first few steps out of her self-made prison. The lady was told about the beautiful dog that had come to visit. "Just come out into the hall and meet him," the staff person said, followed by the little white lie that hospital rules prevented him from entering her room. After some weeping, the lady moved toward the door. The poor soul, longing for some attention and interaction, took a few more desperate steps, totally out of the room. The nurse placed her patient's hand on Teddy's head, and she sat on the floor beside him. To see her petting him, hugging and crying, talking to him at length, was a heartening sight, with lots of wet eyes in the beholders. Staff could hardly believe that this patient had finally found the courage to venture out of her room to be with this lovely dog.

∞ *Pet therapy is a marvelous tonic for aching hearts and hurting spirits, young and old. In family life, dogs can be wonderful ambassadors of good will. A moment of genuine pleasure with the family dog that heals a breached relationship is priceless, indeed, worth all the trouble of keeping a pet.*

⌂ A Dog Named "Jet"

by Rosemary Steele

JET'S LIFE BEGAN IN THE animal sanctuary isolation unit, as one of a litter of puppies that knew absolutely nothing about the outside world. One Saturday, three visitors took a shine to him, calling him Jet because he was swift of paw, though definitely not a high flyer. Jet was just an average-sized mongrel, not outstanding for anything and not overly quick to learn. Nevertheless, Jet had a mission in life, and once he went home with his three new friends, he learned how important his work would be and how wonderful it is to love and be loved.

All three of Jet's new friends are enjoying the "youth of old age," so Jet might well be the last puppy they'll ever have. That's a solemn responsibility. One of them, Mum, is an invalid. Jet spends all day with her, loving, protecting, and giving comfort when needed. What could be more important work? What could be a greater pleasure?

Jet's human dad is quite fit and active. They take long walks together enjoying their man-to-man companionship. The third person in Jet's new world is Aunt Rose, who comes to visit every day and spends her holidays looking after the beloved dog. From the loneliness of the animal shelter to the happiness of a loving home, Jet's travels have made him a most content canine, proud of his human owners, and wishing that all the dogs in the world could be as lucky as he.

⌂ Grip the Altar Boy

by Theresa Mancuso

EVERY SATURDAY EVENING for many years, I drove up the FDR Expressway to East 71st Street to attend vespers service at a small Orthodox church. I always took my dog Grip along for company, as the ride from Brooklyn was rather long. Father Michael allowed me to leave Grip in his office in back of the church rather than outside in the car. The office door remained open during the service, so Grip could see me in the choir stall near the sanctuary.

During the service, when Father Michael walked to the icon stand in the center of the nave, he chanted the prayers while gusts of sweet-smelling incense arose from the golden censer in his hand. Ordinarily, an altar boy would accompany the celebrant and stand beside the priest before the icon, but no altar boy was present this time. As Father Michael approached the icon, Grip quietly arose from his place in back of the church and reverently went to stand beside the priest.

When the worshippers noticed Grip's attempt at being an altar boy, chuckles blended with the sacred chant. I left my place in choir to return Grip to the priest's office. The most unimaginable sweetness appeared in his eyes as he smiled up at me, proudly wagging his tail. "How'd I do, Mom?" Dearest Grip, you did a splendid job, but I'm afraid you just can't be an altar boy.

∞ *As Bishop Sheen always said, "The family that prays together, stays together."*

······································

🏠 Wee Willey Wonka

by Terri J. Stafford

T HEY WERE ASKING TOO MUCH money for the puppies. The pups' living quarters saddened me—dirty, small, no clean water, kibble on the ground. All of them were black except the one I wanted, which had white markings that made him look like he was wearing a tuxedo. Realizing the price was too much, I left disappointed, but several weeks later a friend asked me if I still wanted the pup.

My friend's male had fathered the litter. When my friend discovered that the owner hadn't been able to sell any of the pups and was planning to drown them, he took them all and gave them away to good homes. So we got our puppy and named him Willey.

Although he had an immune deficiency problem, we kept him for our son, Nathan. Soon they became the best of buddies, sleeping together, playing after school, and just hanging out. Willey was a good-natured dog; nothing fazed him. His favorite beverage turned out to be beer, and he would come running when he heard the top popped. One day when Willey was three years old, he suddenly got snappy at the other dogs when they bumped him. The vet's X rays showed that Willey had lymphoma all through him. We took him home for Nathan to say goodbye, and poured Willey his own glass of beer. It took all of his energy to lap it up. We laid Willey to rest at the age of thirty-seven months, a short but happy life.

∞ *Surprises often wait around the next corner so don't let disappointments discourage you. In times of family crises, keep faith with one another and don't give up.*

⌂ Chubby Saves the Day

by Michael Leonard

W HEN MY WIFE AND I WERE YOUNGER, we lived with my parents. My niece and nephew conned my father into buying them a puppy. The new pup was round and sloppy, so we named him Chubby. He lived at Grandma and Grandpa's house, and while he was young, the kids loved to play with him and take care of him. But after six months or so, that black Labrador retriever grew into a full-sized dog, larger than they expected. They still loved playing with Chubby, but they weren't so fond of taking care of him now that he was no longer a puppy.

Grandma and Grandpa had become very fond of Chubby, and they trained him well. He was one of the family. We never expected Grandma to get so attached to a dog. Chubby evolved into a great watchdog for our house and the whole block.

One afternoon, a pack of wild dogs found their way to our neighborhood. They were dangerous. Quickly, the children playing on the sidewalk dispersed. Grandpa didn't like what was happening. A grand master in martial arts himself, Grandpa had taught Chubby how to defend himself. Now it was time to test his skills. When the strays wandered into our back yard through a hole in the fence, Grandpa let Chubby out the back door saying, "Get 'em, Chubby." Chubby quickly dispatched the strays, and the children could play on the sidewalk again without worrying. We were mighty glad they had talked Grandpa into buying that puppy. Chubby saved the day!

∞ *The family pet is often its best protector! If we could be as loving and true to each other as the family dog is to each of us, what wonderful families we would all have.*

🏠 The Locksmith Dog

by Elli Matlin

M Y VERY FIRST GERMAN SHEPHERD bitch was Hexe of Highland Hills, a granddaughter of Irene of Cedarstone, whom we called Reenee. Reenee was known as an escape artist. Reenee would not be kept in a room and could open any door in her path unless it was padlocked. Hexe inherited this trait from her grandmother and took it one step further. Hexe would not only let herself out of any room in the house, and sometimes the house itself, but she would often go from room to room throughout the house and let all the other dogs out also.

Sometimes, like when the PTA ladies were coming over, my mom would put all the dogs out of sight so they wouldn't get dog hair all over their nice clothes. You'd never know when Hexe would decide to open the doors and come strolling out. It was especially funny when she came waltzing into the living room with a litter of puppies bounding after her. Every once in a while the "locksmith gene" reappears in one of Hexe's distant progeny, but we never admit to the puppy owners that we know where it comes from. We simply advise them to use locks with keys.

∞ *If you really want to join the party, find a way to get there.*

⌂ Biting Dog

by Jolanta Benal

W E FOUND OUR SECOND DOG, Muggsy, tied up on our block, and my partner brought him home. He got along with our first dog and didn't eat the cats, so he stayed. But Muggsy bit. He lunged at men in uniform. I found people in uniform who weren't afraid of dogs and walked Muggsy past them, back and forth, feeding him hot dogs and cheese as we slowly got closer. The UPS man and the mailman threw treats from a distance. Soon Muggsy wiggled joyfully when the UPS truck came down the street. We started having guests again.

Over the next year, Muggsy made a new male friend, who promptly dragged our biting dog into his lap and kissed him. I broke out into a cold sweat, but Muggsy wiggled and licked him. The next spring, Muggsy needed a sonogram. The tech suggested sedating him, but I talked her into letting me hold him instead. He lay calmly in the sonogram cradle on his back while a stranger shaved his belly, applied cold gel, and ran the wand over him. I stroked his cheek and talked to him softly. Our biting dog never stirred.

∞ *Perseverance pays. Teaching a difficult child requires great love and patience, but it is worth the effort.*

··

⌂ Family Therapy Should Include the Dog

by Bridgette Mongeon

M Y CHILDHOOD WAS FULL of dysfunction. In fact, even our pet poodle's name, Brandywine, bore evidence to what was happening in our home. My mother was an alcoholic and prescription drug addict. Though Brandywine was the family pet, I always thought of her as Mom's dog.

As the effects of alcoholism ravaged each member of our family, we began to notice a change in Brandy. She cried often, and nothing seemed to soothe her. She just appeared to be very ill. As Mother recalls, "I remember I would lie on the couch, and Brandy would shake in the corner, or under the TV, her eyes just looking at me. Maybe she thought I would fall on her. My heart went out to her, but I could not help myself, much less the dog."

Mother finally "hit bottom" and sought help for her alcoholism. Though it took several years for everyone to adjust to her sobriety, the results in Brandy were astounding. She no longer whimpered when you petted her, and she seemed more relaxed, almost normal.

The incident revealed to me that even family pets are affected by problems within the home. They feel the pain of the loved ones and suffer right along with the entire family. Brandy lived a long and healthy life after that, and Mother has over thirty years of sobriety.

∞ *Healing one helps to heal the many. This is so everywhere, but particularly in the family.*

⌂ The Pitfalls of the Dual-Dog Household

by Barbara Giella, Ph.D.

HAVING MORE THAN ONE DOG is always a challenge, especially when the second dog is foisted on you by your boyfriend and is completely untrained. This story is from my early days as a pack parent, when all I knew was that I didn't know anything.

Our adopted standard poodle, Sasha, used to throw herself at me each time I came home. My Newfoundland, Abby, who also wanted to greet me, would then throw herself on Sasha's back. In a plain attempt to say, "I was here first," Abby would even grab Sasha's skin on the back of the neck while mounting her. I invariably landed on the floor with my purse and packages.

At that time, I was advised to support the dominant dog, but who was it? Damned if I knew.

It didn't matter anyway because Sasha was "inherited" with severe separation anxiety, which boyfriend Jim refused to address. This went on until, fortunately, Jim moved out and peace was restored. Poor Abby, who loved Jim, became an only dog, alas.

∞ *Opposites attract, and difference is an opportunity for learning, but you and your partner need to see eye to eye on some issues if you're going to establish a home together.*

🏠 When a Puppy Dies

by Jack Ryan

JODY WAS PERFECT FOR OUR FOUR YOUNGSTERS, big enough to wrestle and a worthy opponent in tug-of-war. Jody was nonstop motion. That's why it was so alarming one Sunday morning three months after we adopted her, when Jody didn't want to play.

An X ray revealed a large mass. We assumed that she had swallowed a toy or a sock. The vet suggested that we bring Jody in the next day to get spayed and, at the same time, she would open up the stomach.

I brought Jody home and planned to bring her back to the animal hospital the next day. It never happened. I woke up early and found Jody standing in the hallway outside my bedroom. She nuzzled against my leg for a few moments, breathed a last breath, shuddered, and died.

We covered Jody with a blanket and waited until sunrise to break the bad news to the boys. It was their first experience with death. They were heartbroken. Then I made a terrible mistake. I told them they must still go to school, and I would go to work. There was nothing to be gained, I argued, from sitting around feeling sad and angry.

They gave Jody a final kiss and reluctantly went to school. I wrapped Jody in a blanket and took her lifeless body to the vet. An autopsy revealed a cancerous tumor almost never found in pups that young. The boys learned how much it hurts to lose something you love, and I will never be so insensitive again.

∞ *Whatever mistakes we make in life, if we learn from them, they are not tragic. But if we fail to learn, then the harm done is much worse.*

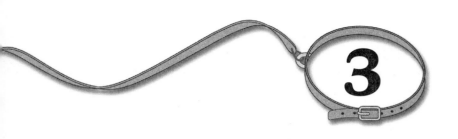

Sniffs and Licks:
Accept Yourself the Way You Are

IN THAT PLACE OF THE HEART WHERE WE are alone with self, we must cast off the opinions of others and come to terms with ourselves. Such purification opens up spiritual resources that define the nature of our experience. It is more about spirit, mind, and free will than physical prowess, appearance, or financial success. Depth of character is the ability to go to the heart of the matter in things that really count. Shallowness cannot travel these deep waters. To see beyond appearances is to grasp the way things really are, and our greatest task in life is simply to understand reality and face it. That is true enlightenment.

By staying still and keeping quiet long enough, we might reach a level of reflection that can penetrate the chaos and noise in our own heads and find the true self within. Sad to say, many of us are just too caught up in externals to deal with a serious and meaningful pursuit of authentic contentment and peace of soul. We seem to get lost in the hubbub of appearances!

Dogs love us unconditionally for who we are. They are singularly incorruptible. Dogs never seem to worry about whether the world likes them or not. Dogs are never phony. By their every action, they tell it like it is. What could be better in the long journey toward acceptance of life as it is than to have such sincere companions? In the anecdotes that follow, we catch a few sniffs and licks that might help us attain a little bit more self-knowledge and acceptance. So, go for it! Fetch! And bring it home!

⌂ Lady in Demand

by Louise Maguire

LADY WAS THE RUNT of a homebred litter of toy spaniels, and she took full advantage of her position. She manipulated humans with her pathetic face, pitiful squeak, and reputation for delicacy. Although officially weaned, she often buffeted her gentle mother, Teala, into letting her take a sly suck or coughing up extra breakfast. While big brothers Charlie and Prince, whom she bullied mercilessly, peacefully slept off a day's mischief, Lady wailed for a cozy human lap and an evening's television viewing.

Lady came to stay with me temporarily, having caused my brother's family more trouble in seven months than her self-effacing mother had managed in four years. Lady dragged Teala out walking by a tender ear, rolled in fox droppings, dived into gorse bushes after rabbits, and wallowed in murky ponds. Teala nurtured slippers; Lady scrunched up pencils, papers, clean clothes, and precious toys. Lady inveigled Teala into imitating garden bookends, terrorizing postmen and passing pedestrians. She wormed her slim body into neighboring gardens, risking death on the road.

Fortunately for her future, Lady settled down and matured with me quite quickly. I would willingly have kept her, but my nieces clamored for her. She returned home at Christmas, an almost reformed character.

Lady repaid her debt the following spring. I borrowed all eighteen pounds of her for a week after my home, where I

---

lived alone, was burglarized. Her alert presence in my room gave me the courage to sleep peacefully at night.

And, of course, she was an excellent reason to acquire a dog of my own.

∞ *Don't fool yourself thinking the smallest is necessarily the least of any litter.*
....

🏠 The Dog Gene

by Theresa Mancuso

I CAN'T REMEMBER A TIME in my life when I didn't want a dog. Not ever. I grew up on stories about Major, a German shepherd that had belonged to Grandpa, whose loyalty and protection was of mythic proportions.

Every birthday and every Christmas, I begged for a dog of my own. I was rebuffed. Dad said, "Ask your mother." Mama said, "*Non c'e necessaria!*" (It isn't necessary, meaning that dogs belong on the farm, not in the house.) Half a century later, the heartache of this scene still resounds in me as if it were yesterday.

I became a nun, and the convent wasn't much better as far as dogs were concerned. When I finally went to the monastery at New Skete, I helped raise German shepherds. But when I left, I continued to have raging puppy hunger. I still do, seven dogs later. I just can't get enough dog.

On the other hand, my brothers and my sister seem capable of life without canines. My sister loves my dogs dearly, but she prefers seeing them *not* in her home territory, an animal-free zone.

So, I ask myself again and again, what is there about dogs and me? I must have the dog gene. I just can't get it out of my system. What about you?

∞ *We are what we are. Some things we can change, and some we can't. The best part of growing older is reconciling ourselves with who we really are and accepting the fact that some things are forever, bred right into our innermost being, down to the quick of us, our DNA, undeniable and absolute.*

 ## ⌂ Charlie

by Heather Cosgrave

WHO KNEW WHEN WE TOOK in Charlie, Manchester terrier, that we would have to deal with such an unfor tunate accident. In doggie rescue work, things happen that we can't predict. Charlie has come such a long way in the time that we've had him, from a scared shadow of a dog that bit if someone reached for him to a loving boy that jumps into the first lap he sees. He struts proudly to get noticed, and if for some reason you aren't paying attention he will jump high into the air until you finally give in and pick him up.

Charlie suffered a severe eye injury last April, and as a result his eye had to be removed. Charlie was so frightened when he arrived at the vet hospital that he had to be sedated. Now he squeals with delight as we turn the corner and runs to the door for that much-anticipated treat waiting inside.

He makes friends everywhere he goes now; he's a new dog.

Charlie has found his forever home now, and he has a new toy Manchester terrier sister, too! He has blossomed into a beautiful, friendly, happy little dog. They told me it would never happen. They told me to give up. But I couldn't. I knew the kind of dog he could be. I was told, "I wouldn't give that dog to my worst enemy." Well, wouldn't they be surprised now?

∞ *In facing life's endless problems and heartaches, challenges, and discouraging moments, never give up or run away. Those who persevere reap the reward of accomplishment and success.*

 A Baby Bird

by Susan Babbitt

JIM AND THE SPRINGER SPANIEL, whom the vet had classified as a "nosy dog," spent numerous miles and hours together walking. They explored a variety of neighborhoods to avoid boredom. On one particular walk, the springer was venturing up onto lawns and under trees capturing interesting smells. As their excursion progressed, Jim became aware of a noise that sounded like chirping. The sound seemed to be traveling with them. The springer appeared oblivious to the noise, continuing his trek onto lawns and under trees as they moved through the neighborhood.

Finally, Jim stopped, commanded his companion to sit, and gently opened the dog's jaws. A small baby bird sat on the springer's tongue, wet from the experience but otherwise unharmed. The dog's passenger was placed under the shelter of nearby foliage, and the afternoon's walk continued. True to his nature, the springer had proven again there was no doubt he was a "bird dog."

∾ *Be your true self. Nature is the defining director of everything we are innately, deep within. Whatever our choices are in life, whatever our efforts to change personality or appearance, the genetic code carried in every cell of our bodies bears the innermost secret of our authentic being.*

⌂ Doggone

by Bridgette Mongeon

O NE DAY I SAW A LITTLE STRAY DOG caught under the fence in my yard. The next day, I saw another large dog hop out of my yard. "What's all the ruckus?" I thought, as I naively brought my white Labrador Casey and retriever Bess from the yard into the house.

Not long after this incident, both of my dogs had puppies. Now we had twenty-one dogs! As they grew, I fed them by filling two wallpaper troughs with food. Having been recently divorced, I was barely able to take care of my daughter and myself. Out of money, in tears, and at my wits' end, I called a local agency. "I have done my best," I explained, "but I need help." They said they only worked with found puppies. Would it be possible for someone to "find" mine? I took my cue! I politely hung up and called right back. "I found nineteen puppies," I said, and they agreed to help.

All the puppies were adopted but one. Each weekend I would take that pup to the adoption pet store in hopes of finding it a home. "What's its name?" they asked. I replied, "I would like to call him 'Gone'." They wrote down: Gone. It took weeks, but by the time the dog was finally adopted his full name was "Doggone-Should-Have-Had-a-Home-by-Now-Brown."

Once I placed all of those puppies in their new homes, every female in my home (with the exception of me and my daughter) was spayed.

∞ *The Lord gives us what we can handle, and sends help when we call out for it.*

 **Rock Star**

by Gabrielle McGhee

L AST OCTOBER, our faithful, ferocious mixed-breed dog Max passed on to his reward in the great dog park in the sky. We grieved and reminisced through the winter, and in springtime, heading home, something made me detour into the driveway of the Stevens Swan Humane Society. "I'll just check out the dogs," I thought, never having discussed with my husband the possibility of taking on another.

The attendant spoke enthusiastically about Star, a German shepherd mix that had been Dog of the Week the month before. Star looked me full in the eye, sitting sedately while all around her yips and howls abounded. Somehow we spoke to each other; she, a middle-aged six-year-old, and I, a middle-aged fifty-three. It felt right that we should get together. I spoke to my husband, and Star and I headed home.

We wondered why her teeth were strangely worn down. Then, one day, our peaceful, crafty girl was let out to investigate our rural lawn and woods. We heard alarming high-pitched shrieks emanating from the back forty and rushed out to see Star hiking a rock like a football, screeching and leaping frenziedly, her front paws pitching the rock backwards as she hopped about.

We soon realized that Star was not about to stop this behavior. She'd happily perform on demand as long as she had a rock large enough to be unchewable, and we thoughtfully provided

---

many. Our rock star happily hiked and called plays for the next seven years.

∞ *The discovery of your hidden talents leads to surprising joys and unexpected delights.*

··

⌂ Tory, My Pal, My Protector

by Elli Matlin

Y EARS AGO, I HAD A GERMAN SHEPHERD named Tory. She was the world's sweetest dog and my first therapy dog. Tory could go anywhere and be with anyone. Though trained in Schutzhund, she thought the whole biting exercise was a big game and never took it seriously. You couldn't make Tory angry.

One day at the vet's office with Tory, I stood behind the counter talking to Kathy, the receptionist. It was fairly late in the evening, and I was waiting for Kathy to count the day's receipts so I could give her a ride home. Into the office strode a man of unsavory character. He began asking strange questions, like how many people were there at that hour. Kathy, feeling the same tension that I did, told him that I was there with "the office guard dog" while she was closing out.

The stranger looked at Tory and said that she looked like an old dog that couldn't do much damage. I responded, "She might be old, but she still has all her teeth." Immediately, Tory stood up, put her front paws on Kathy's desk, and bared every tooth in her mouth. She let out a menacing growl. The man left in a hurry.

I am sure Tory would have followed through on her threat even though it was not her nature to be aggressive.

🐾 *Know what you are capable of, and put forth the effort to do what needs to be done in each circumstance of life. Strive for balance in all things.*

🏠 The Social Director

by Theresa Mancuso

WELL, IF YOU CALLED HER A BUSYBODY, you'd be right. If you called her a pest, you'd also be right. But if you called her the social director, she'd feel a lot better about it. Geisty was an intelligent, lively, and affectionate bitch puppy of five weeks when I brought her home from her litter. Whenever someone spoke to Geisty, she would cock her head to one side as if straining to hear every word and comprehend its meaning. An animal psychic (just like those featured on Animal Planet) told me once that Geisty had almost supernatural powers of hearing, and the evidence convinced me. But Geisty's greatest trait was her dedication to the art of play.

Geisty loved games, no matter what they were or whether she was good at them. Every night she would come to my bed and put a toy on my pillow. If I did not awaken immediately, she returned again and again and again, each time, placing another toy carefully on my pillow. Then she would nudge me with her cold wet nose. If I didn't wake, there was a heavy paw on whatever part of my body she could reach. Geisty could have been a twenty-four-hour tireless working dog.

When Geisty mothered a litter of seven puppies, she became their play director. She would roll over on her back and toss toys up into the air for them to catch. The more they scrambled after the toys she tossed, the happier she was.

∞ *Play is necessary throughout our lives to restore our inner selves and create the bonds of community with others. Play is therapeutic and educational.*
....

⌂ A Good Dog in Any Language

by Heather Pate

ONE DAY, OUR REGIONAL TELEVISION station's thirty-minute weekday magazine show featured a segment on a deaf Dalmatian female named Wonder. One of the volunteer dog walkers at the local SPCA shelter took Wonder on as a special project and taught her a variety of hand signals, such as sit, down, walk nicely on a leash, and do a short stay.

My three Great Danes, Loki, Tuni, and Chance, were riveted to the television during this segment. Chance is deaf, and she saw Wonder's human friend give the "Sit" sign, a different one than I use. Then Wonder got her "Good dog" sign, the thumbs-up that means "good" in American Sign Language. Chance went into hyper alert, with her nose almost touching the television screen. Next, Wonder was told "Down," and the sign used was the same one I use. Chance dropped to the floor in a perfect down. Both Chance and Wonder got their "Good dog" thumbs-up sign. Chance's tail was wagging fiercely, and she turned to me as if to say, "Hey! That lady on the TV is talking to ME!"

There were absolutely no cues from me to elicit this behavior. But "Good dog" in any language makes for a happy canine!

∞ *Whatever we may lack in life can be compensated for in terms of how much we try to do our best with whatever we have.*

🏠 A Dog Named Woof

by Marcy Rauch

WOOF WAS THE KIND OF DOG that comes along once in a lifetime. She took life head-on with great determination. Woof was deaf, yet she shattered the boundaries of her silent world with what she could do. She learned agility at twelve years young and herded sheep for the first time at eleven. A quadriplegic from tick paralysis, Woof learned to stand again. When others missed a fallen biscuit, Woof saw it and with sheer determination, forced herself up to get it. She taught children that deaf dogs are special and brought tears to the eyes of one deaf child who felt alone in her plight. During her last year, confined to a wheelchair, Woof showed her mettle by hiking, swimming, and never giving in to defeat. She had a wheelchair race with a boy suffering from spina bifida. He won by a hair. In Woof's last outing, she shared what she had left with a young man suffering from cerebral palsy.

This is what legends are made of. People asked me how I kept her going so long. My answer was that as long as Woof was smiling, I would do whatever it took to keep her going. She stopped smiling one Sunday night. Two days later, with great sadness, I helped her leave the body that had given up on her. Woof and I were together for fifteen years. Sleep well, my friend. Your spirit and strength are in my heart forever.

∞ *We must face our lives as they are. The greatest challenge of all is to take what we have been given and do our best with it.*

⌂ The Story of Benny

by Danielle Wiley

F OUND WANDERING IN NORTHERN MICHIGAN with a bloody leg and a dazed look in his eyes, he was brought to the pound that had the highest kill rate in the state. To this day, no one can explain why or how. Despite his advanced age (he was probably about eight years old) and his severe leg wound, his life was spared, and Michigan Weimaraner Rescue was called. We adopted him in August of 2000.

Benny was only with us for ten short months, but he changed our lives. We know that his life before us was a hard one. There were scars around his neck where a prong collar must have once grown into the skin, and his almost desperate need for love made it clear that it was something he had never known.

Just a few months after we got him, we discovered that Benny had mast cell cancer. When it spread to his brain and began affecting his ability to get around without pain, we made the toughest decision of our lives. That night, my husband suggested that we write up "The Tao of Benny." Here, then, are some of the life rules that Benny taught us.

∞ *Be grateful for the good, not angry at the bad. Don't let the past get in the way of today. Physical scars need not destroy your inner spirit. A few well-timed kisses mean a lot. It's the little things that make life great. Don't bark unless it's absolutely necessary. Always be grateful for a good meal. Never forget to smile.*

⌂ The Good Bitch

by Brenda Abbott

ALL DOG PEOPLE KNOW WHAT A "GOOD BITCH" is, and some people even own one! You know the good bitch . . . she's the one who can be trusted in any circumstance. She stays in the car full of groceries while you run into the post office and never touches a bag. She sleeps loose in the house or the RV and never makes a mess. Trashcans are even safe from the good bitch. Here's the best "good bitch" story I've ever heard, from longtime Samoyed breeder, Frances Powers.

Frances and a friend had gone to a dog show with several dogs. They checked into their motel room and moved several dog crates into the room. They were one crate short for the number of dogs they had with them, but that was no problem because in this group was the good bitch, and she could certainly be left loose! When Frances and her friend decided to go out for a quick dinner, all of the dogs were given a safe chew bone, and the door was closed. An hour later, Frances and her friend returned to find all dogs peacefully sleeping, including the good bitch, settled in atop one of the beds. The two humans gathered leashes and collars to take the pack out for a walk, and the "good bitch" stood up and stretched . . . to reveal a two-foot-wide hole in the motel's mattress, where she had "buried" her bone!

∞ *There's some good in the worst of us and there's some bad in the best of us, so that behooves none of us to talk about the rest of us.*

⌂ Bridgett Shows Her True Colors

by Dr. Muriel Beerman

ONE MORNING AS MY FIVE DOGS and I traveled our usual route in Brooklyn, we came to the park that is our turnaround point for our hour walk.

Normally, in the early hours before 6 A.M., we see very few people on our jaunt and even fewer dogs. But that day,

I spotted an Akita running in the park. I wasn't worried because the iron fence around the park appeared to be secure, and the front gate was locked. But then the Akita squeezed between the bars, crossed the avenue, and came straight for my girls. He bounded up to us and picked the most timid of my Labs, JJ, to intimidate. He began to snarl. At that moment, my best-behaved Lab, Bridgett, pulled her leash out of my hands and began to circle our group. She strutted between the Akita and our group, almost pushing her body between my terrified JJ and this strange intruder. Bridgett kept circling us, making herself as big as she could.

It worked. The Akita backed off. The owner ran up to us apologizing. She leashed her dog and was off.

Bridgett had never done anything like that before. She never pulled away from me and never showed any kind of bravery before. But she knew that we needed her.

∞ *When the time comes, muster up all your courage and know you can overcome every obstacle to do the right thing.*

 Oops!

by Dr. Nancy Bekaert

CLIENTS SOMETIMES ASK ME TO CHOOSE a puppy for them: "We want a friendly, outgoing female German shepherd." I reported this to my friend, who had a litter of twelve six-week-old pups. I spent several hours evaluating them and chose the smallest, brightest, most outgoing female.

Returning home, I called the clients to let them know they'd have their pup shortly. They were ecstatic.

I taped my entire drive from home to the kennel. Dolly, as they planned to name her, dashed to the kennel door to greet me. I told her that she was going to a wonderful home in Brooklyn. Dolly scooted into the carrier and handled the three-hour drive like a seasoned traveler.

When we finally reached our destination, I honked the horn. The video was still running as I followed the action. Her excited owners ran out to get her crate, carried it into the house, and opened it. After kisses and squeals of delight from both pup and owners, Dolly rolled over on her back for a tummy rub. Oops, wrong puppy! It seems that "Dolly" was really a "Donald"—or rather a Stuart Little, as it turned out.

∞ *Mistakes can sometimes have a happy ending.*

 Happy Baby

by Theresa Mancuso

AFTER RUNNING MY DOGS in a remote field on the edge of Brooklyn one summer night, I was putting them up in my van when I noticed a dark shadow scamper into the abandoned hangar. I could just make out the dim visage of a small black pit bull staring back at me from behind a pillar. I called out, "Come on out, little one, it's okay." No response.

Procuring an extra dog dish, I brought her water, and began bringing her food and water every morning and every evening.

When there was sufficient distance between us, she would emerge from the shadows and eat and drink with one eye watching me.

A week had passed when a trooper told me that animal control had been called about the "dangerous stray pit bull."

I came back the next morning, held my breath, said a prayer, and squatted low. "Come on, Baby. This is it." She flew into my embrace. I removed the couple dozen swollen ticks that were embedded in her body, wiped her down with baby wipes, and put a collar and leash on her. Then I went to the main office. The trooper told me I was putting myself in grave danger. "She's mine, Officer," I told him, as she licked my face joyously. "I'm taking her home." And off we went directly to my vet's office.

Happy Baby was soon placed in a loving home with a family in Westchester.

∞ *Let your love and kindness draw unto you the poor, the needy, the dispossessed and all those who need your friendship.*

⌂ Emmy's Vigilance

by Mike de la Flor

EMMY, OUR GERMAN SHEPHERD, had suddenly become protective of my wife, Bridgette. She began to shadow my wife's every move. During walks in the park, even when off her leash, Emmy would not stray more than a few feet. A few weeks later, to our surprise, we discovered we were pregnant.

Then one day Emmy's behavior changed again. During her daily walk, Emmy strayed far and resumed her old foraging behavior. Bridgette came home visibly upset and said, "Something's wrong; Emmy won't have anything to do with me." I reassured her, and asked her not to worry.

Days later we went in for a scheduled ultrasound. Though we could see the fetus on the screen, there was no sound. The doctor sighed and broke the terrible news, "We can't locate a heartbeat. The baby has died. I am very sorry." My wife and I were devastated. It was the saddest day of our lives.

We don't know how, but Emmy had sensed my wife's pregnancy before we knew, and she instinctively protected her master in this delicate condition. Sadly, Emmy was also the first to know that our baby had died. In her own way, Emmy shared in our joy and sadness.

∞ *Real love and care is the route to understanding ourselves and others.*

⌂ The Annual Birthday Bash

by Paul Sutton

O N AUGUST 16, 1995, my Border collie, Whisper, had seven puppies. I kept two. Three others live locally.

Each year they have a birthday party complete with hats, in a different style every year. The party starts with hat time. I keep the hats a secret in order to get the adults' reaction as I put them on each dog in turn. There are shrieks of "Oooo!" and "Aah!" and much hysterical laughter. For dogs to sit still wearing hats for several minutes is quite a triumph.

Once the hats are all on—and they *never* try to knock them off—the cameras are in frantic action, like a press photo call for celebrities. The dogs sit patiently waiting for all of us to get that special shot. Sunny stands out, for he is the biggest poser and the camera loves him. He could have been a model.

When photo call is over, it's cake time, a mixture of vegetables, rice, and ground meat in a big baking tray. There are candles on the cake and everybody sings Happy Birthday. The neighbors in all likelihood think that I am mad, but I bet they also get a laugh when they look out their windows. All of the dogs tuck their heads into the bowl together to eat their cake from the same dish without a murmur of protest.

At the end of the evening, the birthday dogs go home with a party bag full of goodies, no doubt ready for a good night's sleep after all the excitement.

∞ *It's the eccentrics that make the rest of us look more or less normal.*

⌂ Tot, the Hero

by Jenny Moir

TOT, AN EIGHT-YEAR-OLD Yorkshire terrier, was just another young fellow waiting to be adopted out from Battersea Dogs' Home, when the charity Hearing Dogs for Deaf People selected him for four months of training in sound work. In February 1997, the charity placed Tot with Julia, who had been profoundly deaf more than forty years.

Tot has become Julia's ears and has changed her life. Her confidence soars. She trusts him to alert her to the doorbell and the phone. He also knows a special procedure for sounds that signify danger, such as the smoke alarm or the fire bell.

Tot's sunny personality is an extra. "Tot smiles all the time," Julia says with pride. "I tell the children he meets that if they say hello to him, he will smile . . . and he does!"

Recently, Tot rescued Julia's husband, too. Joe had just come out of hospital, and Julia moved into another room to sleep so she wouldn't disturb him at night. One night, Joe collapsed on his way to the bathroom. Julia heard nothing at all, but little Tot came to the rescue. He ran to find Julia, scrabbled at her until she woke up, and then led her into the bathroom where she discovered Joe unconscious on the floor. Tot saved Joe's life.

∞ *Even the smallest creatures have value and valor.*

🏠 The Guide Dog That Sucked His Thumb

by Pat Hill

RAYMIE, SHORT FOR RAYMOND, is a large black Lab with a lovely wavy coat. He has a large head, broad shoulders, and gentle, expressive brown eyes. Raymie is my current guide dog, and though he's a very serious worker, he also has an impeccable sense of humor. We were still in training when I discovered this.

During training, I also discovered a rather unique habit Raymie had at night—chewing his own foot. I checked his foot and could not find any break in his pads or anything stuck to them, so I asked an instructor if she could see anything. The instructor checked Raymie's paw and didn't find a problem. She watched him walk and saw no change in his gait, no limp or other difficulty. Just to be on the safe side, the instructor asked the vet to check him. The vet could find nothing wrong with him either, but he suggested that whenever I heard Raymie chewing on his foot, I should tell him to stop, which he did.

A few weeks later when I met the woman who had raised Raymie, I asked her about this peculiar habit. That's when I learned that Raymie had always sucked his paw when he went to bed at night. It was something he did every night as a puppy and still does today, at age seven.

∞ *Some habits are lifelong in duration. There are times when it is better to make peace with our idiosyncrasies than to loathe eccentricities we cannot overcome.*

Give a Paw:
Getting Along with Others

ONE GREAT THING ABOUT DOGS is the way they get along with people and other dogs. Most puppies will rush up to everyone as if to say, "Hi, I'm Puppy Little. Who are you?" Even jumping up on people is a manifestation of their complete willingness and inclination to make friends.

Our social nature requires interaction and cooperation. It's a lifelong challenge to get along with people. You know the old quip, "I love mankind; it's people I can't stand."

Dogs teach us a great deal about getting along with others. When they spot one another on a busy street, in the park, or at the beach, their automatic reflexes rev up. They bark. They wag their tails. They lift their ears and their noses wiggle. They want to meet and greet, sniff and play.

Dog aggression is an undesirable trait. Often, it's reason enough to return a puppy. People aggression is just as distasteful. When we indulge judgmental, critical, or unaccepting attitudes, we give expression to something that is very unlovable in ourselves. Is it greed? Is it suspicion? Is it narcissism?

Dogs are prone to give a paw almost universally. Habitual paw-givers show that they have learned the fine art of meeting people with openness and sincerity. We can do it, too, and it goes a long way to making life worth living.

The pure of heart, the peacemakers, the meek, and all those of good will are blessed indeed. All spiritual paths commend sincerity of heart and authentic love for the neighbor. I often think that dogs seem to get it right the first time around, while we seem to stumble along our whole lives trying to understand and practice the principles of spiritual wholeness. The stories in this chapter will inspire us to do better in getting along with others, so open up your heart and give a paw!

⌂ To Err Is Human, but Canines Are Divine

by Maxine Perchuk

U NLIKE THE HUMAN CHILDREN of some other mothers, my canine children are well behaved and possessed of a healthy sense of shame. Parents of human children often look at my basset and terrier with suspicious and judgmental gaze, while their own children make barking noises at my two bewildered babes who nonetheless sit calmly and quietly observing. At times, a child has attempted to stamp or swipe at one of my dogs, and I have had to intervene. On one such occasion, a mother yelled at me for daring to raise my voice to her little darling.

My basset hound, Beatrice, has the good grace to lower her head and feverishly twitch the tip of her tail when she knows she's misbehaved. Recently I came home from work to find an odoriferous pile—a protest from Bea at having been left behind all day.

Willie, my terrier, was carefree, but Bea would not look my way. When I questioned her, the tip of her tail started to beat wildly as if involuntarily, further incriminating her. I know that I probably gave her the wrong message when I kissed her pointed head and embraced her, but a healthy sense of guilt is so endearing that I find myself utterly disarmed. She would prefer not to address her earlier actions, but unlike so many humans who are capable of heaping piles of denial, she gives herself away.

∞ *It's easier to forgive someone who shows remorse.*

Gallo

by Susan Babbitt

G ALLO DE LOS PAJAROS was a liver-and-white registered English springer spaniel. He joined our family while I was in high school. Early every morning, my father ventured into the kitchen and, while looking out the kitchen window, would blow his nose. Frequently, while perusing the back yard at that early hour, Dad would see a cat, and he would alert Gallo. Gallo would run through the house and out the dog door to rid the premises of the intruder. Eventually, Gallo began to run out to the back yard to protect his territory whenever Dad blew his nose, regardless of where Dad was in the house, or what time of day it was.

My brother, Jim, took special pleasure in dressing Gallo in gym shorts, T-shirts, and sweat socks, and then telling him to go find Mom. Gallo would advance into whatever room Mom was in, head hung low as if in embarrassment, tail wagging, knowing he had obeyed his orders. Mom would then praise Gallo and tell him how handsome he was, what a truly good boy he was, all the while undressing him. All three of them greatly enjoyed this game.

∞ *Take your cues where you find them, and do your best to make things work.*

⌂ A Jack Russell Tale

by Kerry Dahlheim

I HAVE BEEN DOING JACK RUSSELL terrier rescue for about seven years now. We bought our first Jack Russell terrier at seven weeks of age and adopted our second one at a year and a half. He was the one that got me started doing rescue work.

To date, I have rescued over a hundred dogs, and I could tell you a story about each one of them. Some bring laughter into my house, and some bring sadness. I have had to heal dogs through heartworm treatment, a difficult challenge. But I think that each of them comes into my life for a reason.

The dogs I rescue teach me many things. For example, puppy-mill dogs we have rescued taught me patience. It's so nice to visit them in their new homes. I love to watch them when they see and then recognize my face again, their bodies wiggling with excitement telling me that I have placed them in a great home. Some of these new places are truly homes fit for a king. Rescue work can be very rewarding. I often get e-mails from new dog owners thanking me for the wonderful pet that I brought into their lives. There is a saying I use a lot in this work: "Someone's trash is someone else's treasure."

∞ *The good things we do enhance the world in which we live; whether acknowledged or not, every act of kindness counts.*

 **Full House**

by Deborah Palman

K EEPING AND TRAINING SEVERAL POLICE or Schutzhund dogs inside your home is not easy. Dogs meant to do protection work are bred to be pain tolerant and have high drives to eat, to chase moving objects, and to establish themselves as high as possible in the pack pecking order. These characteristics are great if you're a police officer and a criminal is assaulting you, but a house full of working dogs definitely makes home life more difficult. I've had many experiences that bear witness to this fact. The working breeds sometimes get a bad reputation for not getting along with others, but it's that same genetic makeup that makes them such good workers.

I found that I could easily keep working dogs of the opposite sex together, or a mother and her female offspring together, but not indefinitely. People who have kept a mother and daughter together for more than three years say that eventually, the daughter will fight with the mother for dominance. This usually happens after about four or five years, as the mother gets older and the daughter reaches her prime. Much of the strength in strong working females is created by a strong sense of self and desire to dominate. Submissive working dogs don't bite and fight with criminals, so they are selected out of the gene pool. Dogs communicate with others constantly through eye contact and body postures. Owners need to observe and learn this language to be fair and just pack leaders, intervening when trouble erupts.

⊗ Strong-willed individuals tend to butt against one another, but insight and wisdom enables us to grow in strength and still get along with others.
....

 ## Bullet

by Barbara Croke

I N APRIL OF 2001, I BROUGHT HOME a four-week-old male puppy, a German shepherd/Akita mix. I named him Bullet. His mother had abandoned him, along with the rest of her litter. He wasn't able to eat dog food yet, so for a few weeks I fed him Esbilac (milk replacement for puppies) and gradually weaned him to dog food.

Bullet didn't have all of his shots, so I kept him in the yard away from other dogs until he was fully vaccinated. When I first began to walk him, Bullet was afraid of trucks, cars, and motorcycles. He would stop and refuse to walk any further until I told him it was okay. In time, he has overcome his fear of trucks and cars, but when he hears a motorcycle, he still stops and watches it until it passes by him. When Bullet hears thunder or a helicopter, he leans against me until I tell him it's okay.

Although Bullet is not the world's bravest dog, he's my companion, and I love him. He follows me wherever I go in the house. When I sit, he has to lie down near my feet or take a seat at my side—he loves to lean on me. Not everyone requires a macho dog. For me, Bullet is the best of the best.

∞ Mutual love and respect are the foundation for getting along with others. It doesn't matter whether the world approves or appreciates the ties that bind you to the ones you love. Getting along together is not about what others think; it's all about what you think and what you do.

⌂ Dog of Destiny

by Enid Coel

W HEN FLETCHER DIED, I THOUGHT MY world would become a feline kingdom, for I was a cat rescuer. Fletcher had been a stubborn dog. Perhaps he had no choice, living as he had with seven cats for fourteen years. A mousy-brown Chihuahua mix, Fletcher never yielded to human authority, and being small of stature, he got away with his rebellions.

Some months after Fletcher's decease, I accompanied a friend to a Brooklyn animal shelter, a place of heartbreak as well as opportunity. There, dogs and cats get a second chance and even a third for a new home, but if they're not adopted, it's doomsday. Having been "fletchered" for fourteen years, I was amazed to find myself falling in love with a small gray dog being dropped off at the shelter by his family, now abandoning him.

That's how Meiko came into my life, a poodle/Shih Tzu mix with such a keen intelligence that it amazes me every single day. I lifted Meiko atop the radiator cover in the lobby of our building one rainy day, to towel him off. He licked my face expectantly and from that day forth, Meiko leaps onto the radiator cover whenever we return from a wet walk in snow or rain. He thinks my friend's blue Subaru Forester, in which he rode home the day I adopted him, is partly "his car," so he leaps in with delight every chance he gets. Meiko adores his sibling cats, strutting proudly through their midst, Mr. Big, Dog of Destiny!

∞ *You never know how your heart will expand to let in one more.*

⌂ Mister's Broken Heart

by Elli Matlin

M ISTER AND MISSUS WERE OUR TWO adopted strays. We often called them our Sloman's Shield, after the home security system, because they were so protective of our property.

Mister and Missus lived contentedly on our front porch in doghouses we bought for them for over ten years. When Missus got to be about sixteen, she became more and more arthritic. Last fall, she started losing weight and hair and didn't look good. I feared she would not make it through the winter and considered putting her down, but I didn't because I knew what it would do to Mister.

The decision was taken out of my hands the next fall, when Missus died on her own. I tried to bring Mister into the house, so he could bond with one of my housedogs, but he would have no part of it. Mister retreated into Missus's dog-house on the porch, lay down, and refused to leave. He wouldn't eat or do anything. I knew he was mourning for Missus and tried to convince him to take his favorite snacks, but he ate very little and finally, nothing at all. Mister passed away barely three weeks after Missus did, I'm sure of a broken heart. Even though we had predicted that Mister could not survive without his Missus, I never thought he'd just give up and die that quickly. Now, let us hope, they are reunited at the Rainbow Bridge.

∞ *True love lasts forever.*

⌂ Pack Buddy Telepathy

by Dottie Seuter

A BOUT TWENTY YEARS AGO, our twelve-year-old German shepherd bitch Happy suddenly stopped eating. She had never missed a meal in her entire life, so I knew something must be seriously wrong even though she had no other obvious symptoms.

I took her to our vet the next morning and she was diagnosed as having hemolytic anemia. The veterinarian felt that her prognosis was not very promising, but he said that if we wanted him to do so, he would try to treat her day by day to see if he could get her a bit more quality time before the end came. For a few days it seemed as if it might work. When I went to visit her, she was obviously feeling better and cleaning up her food. I felt a glimmer of hope.

The next day was Sunday, and at about 7:30 in the morning, my eight-year-old German shepherd male suddenly started howling. Fifteen minutes later, the vet tech called to tell me that Happy was dead. When I asked him when she had died, he said it was just about 7:30 that morning.

I will always believe that Butch knew the moment she died and that was why he was so upset.

∞ *The bonds of friendship last and manifest in ways that are often mysterious and marvelous.*

🏠 Motivating Beatrice

by Theresa Mancuso

M Y FRIEND MAX AND I frequently take our dogs to Floyd Bennett Field to play search and rescue games. Neither Maxine nor I are trained search-and-rescue handlers, but we love playing the game, and we actually have worked our way through a book of search-dog training exercises.

My German shepherds, Grip, Geisty, and Abby, and Max's terrier mix, Wilhelmina, tear into action as soon as they are released. "Go 'Find,'" I say, and they will not be stopped until they find the "victim." Then they return to show us where the hider is. Beatrice, Max's basset hound, on the other hand, stands and bays until the search begins, at which point she meanders nonchalantly in whatever direction strikes her fancy.

We succumbed to bribing the wayward Bea with sausage treats. Bea needed but to sniff the contents of the little sack we carried when we went to hide. From the moment we implemented the sausage routine, Bea led the way, a champion search dog, up for any challenge, fast as a comet plunging through the thicket in search of the "victim"—well, not the victim, perhaps, but certainly the sausage.

∞ *Noble motivations are best, but sometimes just getting a simple task done is worthy enough incentive to support the cooperative effort.*

....

⌂ Rohn Takes the Lead

by Lynzie Bacchus

ONE OF OUR FEMALE ALASKAN HUSKIES, Dallas, was bred to our male, River. Dallas had a litter of seven puppies, but one of them died. When the puppies got to about three months old, two more of them became ill and had to be put down. There were only four pups left. We gave one away and I kept two males, Rylee and Rohn.

I knew there was something special about Rohn and thought that one day he would be a great asset to my kennel. At the age of only six months, although ordinarily too young to be the leader, Rohn took to leading my dogsled team like a natural. He was such a powerhouse that I loved having him up front.

When we raced in the Junior Iditarod, I put Rohn in the lead position. At only a year old, Rohn led the whole way. If it wasn't for him, we would not have crossed the finish line, but we did. Rohn just stepped up during the last twenty miles and became a real leader.

∞ *Leadership comes from within. It rises to the surface when circumstances call it forth. It takes the lead when others need to follow.*
·················

♠ On the Job with Officer Abby

by Theresa Mancuso

S OCIALIZATION IS AN ABSOLUTELY ESSENTIAL aspect of puppy rearing. If you do it right and temperament is normal, you should have a friendly, outgoing dog like my Abby. Wherever she goes, Abby seems to think that the whole world's her family, and every place is her playground. Along with the New York City Department of Probation, where I have worked for all of Abby's life, the NYPD sponsors family-day picnics in high-crime neighborhoods. Abby accompanies me enthusiastically. I think she fancies herself a probation officer. Inevitably, she becomes a star attraction, as kids surround us and ask if they can hold her leash. She licks faces and gives her paw with tireless good will. Neither summer heat nor sudden storms deter this devoted canine.

Then one year word went out that no dogs would be permitted at the family day being held in an East New York field. Abby looked forlorn when I loaded up my gear and said goodbye that Saturday morning.

Just about eleven o'clock, I saw a woman standing inside the main gate with a large black Labrador. "Hmmm," I reflected. "I better warn her that no dogs are allowed." As I approached the woman, she turned and smiled.

Whoops. "Good morning, Mrs. Commissioner, how are you today?"

The commissioner's wife greeted me; her big black Lab offered me a paw!

Ꮟ *Don't be too eager to enforce rules that interfere with your plans. Do what you have to do, and mind your business!*

⌂ The Taming of Tiger

by Louise Maguire

AT FIRST I PITIED THE SCRAP of a rescued cat, no bigger than a kitten, that moved in next door. Sadly, Tiger turned into a tabby tyrant, and my collies, Cindy and Juli, became his favorite victims. He terrorized the well-trained pair, ambushing them from rose beds or pouncing down from windowsills.

Tiger gradually took possession of the shared garden. Then our communal hall became forbidden territory when Tiger prowled the stairs. Finally, they could scarcely take refuge anywhere, trembling on their own doorstep.

I found myself treated as an honorary canine, hissed at by the menacing feline.

Then my brother's toy spaniels, Teala and her tough daughter, Lady, came as guests on holiday. Cindy's large dog bed was usurped at once. Lady enthroned herself on a scraped-up pile of blankets for the duration, while Teala and Cindy were shoehorned into a basket designed for two toy spaniels. Juli, Cindy's young half sister, was duly quashed. She kowtowed visibly though she was at least three times Lady's size.

As for spitting, bristling Tiger, Lady chased him three times around our block of flats, and then followed him when he retreated onto the back of a garden seat. The forsythia bush he leaped into next was just too much for Lady's short legs, if not her gallant spirit.

Lady dusted off her paws and popped into the kitchen to see what goodies she could pinch to build up her eighteen-pound frame for the next event.

∞ *Bullies, beware! Someone tougher than you might be just around the corner!*

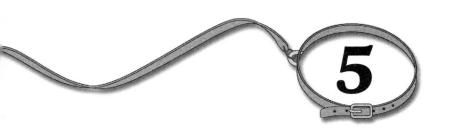

Lick the Bowl Clean:
Make the Best of Things

DOGS AT THEIR FOOD BOWLS SHOW US exactly what it means to make the best of things. They guzzle down whatever we offer, making us wonder where it goes with so much speed. Immediately after wolfing down a meal, dogs lick their bowls so clean, they look as if they just came out of a dishwasher. Given the opportunity, family dogs love nothing better than permission to carry out mop-up operations in the kitchen, licking pans and serving bowls. If by chance the folks are really easygoing, the crème de la crème moment is when their laid-back owners finish a meal and lower their plates to the floor, so the canine caterers can rush in and lick them clean.

You don't have too many finicky dogs out there hesitating or turning up their noses at what we dish out to them, but me, oh my! How we humans do turn up our noses when life dishes out a less than palatable situation. What to do?

Why, do as the dogs do, of course! Take it as it comes. Ingest reality, digest it, and assimilate it. Make it your own.

If we could glean from our dogs a little of their superb ability to make do and accept whatever morsels of reality life dishes out to us, enjoying them to the fullest, chewing on them contemplatively, sucking up the juices and the marrow—hey, we'd be making the best of everything! Dogs take the whole of life and "lick the bowl clean." Would that we could, too. Whatever it is you're facing this very moment, take a lesson from your dog! Make the best of it! Strive to be happy!

⌂ Dog People and Non-Dog People

by Robert Frenzel-Berra

A WHAT?" I SAID IN BEWILDERMENT.
"You know," she said. "A dog." My wife wanted a dog.

I had to think about what was being said here. Pause. Concentrate. My wife and I stared at each other across the great chasm that separates the human race into two classes, dog people and non-dog people.

I wonder if there might be a specific gene for "dog person." Some people who never had a dog when they were growing up are smitten later in life by the puppy in the window, the old yeller feller in the park, or that remarkably friendly, intelligent, and healthy dog in the movie. And real dog people never mind when the dog they get pees and poops in the house, growls, barks all night, sheds, or chews up the leather couch.

For dog people, the pleasure of owning a dog outweighs all the hassles.

But I've never even felt that pull. You can easily imagine the challenges to a relationship when one partner is a dog person and the other is not. Although it may not be possible to eradicate the divide that separates them, bridges of sorts can be built.

And my wife and I stumbled along until we got Conrad, a throwback American cocker spaniel.

∞ *When you can't see eye-to-eye, look for compromises. If you can't accept compromise, you're in big trouble!*

🏠 Clean Sheets

by Theresa Mancuso

I T'S AN OLD ADAGE THAT CLEANLINESS is next to godliness. Perhaps, in the mind of my dog Grip, the saying ought to have been "Cleanliness is next to dogliness."

Grip loved clean sheets. He liked them on his platform bed in the back of the van, nicely tucked around its padded sleeping-bag cover. He liked them tossed over the couch in the living room where he spread out to relax after a doggone busy day. He liked them in his crate, wrapping the foam mattress into a neat rectangle of canine comfort. But most of all, Grip loved cool, clean sheets on Mom's bed.

Every time I changed my bedding, the same thing happened, and more than once, I witnessed this particularly interesting maneuver. I'd clean the bedroom thoroughly, change the bed, and then move along through the apartment doing other chores. Inevitably, at some point after I had installed clean sheets on my bed, I'd catch sight of Grip, often from the far end of the apartment, just coming up on the screen of my peripheral vision.

Grip would make a gingerly leap, ninety-six pounds of German shepherd manliness, up to the top of the bed, where he patiently turned back the comforter using his front paws, and then snuggled down into the clean sheets, his head on my pillow, a very happy dog.

∞ *Learn to take pleasure in small things.*

⌂ A Day of Destiny

by Edy Makariw

M Y MOTHER WAS ON HER WAY OVER for her first extended visit in several years. After meeting her at the station, we strolled about pleasantly and ended up at the farmers' market at Union Square in Manhattan. I don't think that either of us had ever seen so many raspberries! What a delight they were, sweet and slightly warm at the end of a late summer afternoon. Mom and I, and several pints of raspberries, sat out the quickly approaching thunderstorm in a cozy Chinese restaurant while we enjoyed a light dinner. I mentioned to her that we must shortly head for home. After all, I said, the dogs must be walked, mustn't they?

The next day, we planned to see an art exhibit in downtown Manhattan. A friend of mine had recommended it, and why not have breakfast first, at a coffee shop I'd always been meaning to try? The coffee shop was located in the ground level of the World Trade Center. The plan had been to ride into the city with my partner, who worked in midtown Manhattan. But Mom and I wanted to have a casual start to the day, so we decided to maintain our relaxed pace and let my partner go on ahead. Taking care of the canines first, we were delayed getting into New York.

The date was September 11, 2001, and we were not among the people having latte and croissants at the World Trade Center because, after all, the dogs had to be walked, didn't they?

∞ *Meeting your obligations can be more valuable than you expect.*

🏠 A Suicide Watchdog

by Neal C. Jennings

A DOG CAN BE A GUIDE DOG, a watchdog, a hearing ear dog, a therapy dog, a seizure dog, or a drug-sniffing dog, but few have heard of a suicide watchdog. A few years ago, an elderly gentleman met with the manager of the Scottsdale Civic Senior Center, in Arizona.

He said he had a dog story that he believed reached the peak of human-animal communications. He had been despondent over recent losses, both of loved ones and material things. At the time of his greatest depression, he brought his gun into the living room, loaded it, and readied himself to put an end to his troubles.

While he was lining up the barrel for a hit to the most vital spot, the steady gaze of the dog at his feet caught his attention. In that moment, he related, the dog looked at him as if to say, "Okay, what is it we're going to do now? What's going to happen to me?" His intense train of thought was broken. At that moment, he moved out of his horrible nightmare and suddenly realized that he still had love and responsibility. He put down the gun and began to re-examine his life.

Then he said to the senior center's manager, "As a start, I have come to volunteer my time and services to others. Tell me what I can do to help."

∽ *When you lose heart about the way things are, remember those who care for you and need you. Thinking of others is the best way to heal yourself.*

⌂ The Scalping of Meiko

by Enid Coel

M Y POODLE-MIX PUP WAS NOT QUITE this and not quite that, but he was a handsome dude all the same. Whatever he was, he certainly had strong coat genes floating around in his DNA, because he just got furrier and furrier, curlier and curlier. Several months after I adopted him, I asked a friend and fellow dog-lover to help me trim Meiko's overgrown coat.

Sitting out in the summer sun one day at our favorite doggie haunt, I rummaged through my bag and found a small inadequate pair of scissors. What luck! Hair by hair, my friend began to "trim" Meiko's coat, but alas, the trimming was, in fact, a scalping of my poor pup. He sat peacefully unaware as I held him gently in my arms, assuring him that he was the most perfect, the most beautiful, the most wonderful guy in all of dogdom. Lucky for us, there wasn't a mirror in sight and as I don't have mirrors at dog level in my home, Meiko never fully grasped the primitive scalping his haircut turned out to be.

Offering not a gesture or bark of reproof or resistance, but with exquisite patience and humility, Meiki dutifully accepted the work of our hands as we traversed his body and rearranged his God-given coat. A clip here, a clip there, many clips everywhere. Soon, he took on the appearance of an altogether new breed. Despite it all, Meiko stood tall in the aftermath, while my friend and I quietly retired from the grooming business.

∞ *External beauty is a combination of good fortune and*

---

endurance, but internal beauty is a spiritual thing that comes
from a clear conscience and acceptance of one's place in the
universe.
··············

⌂ The Baby Prince

by Dottie Seuter

MANY YEARS AGO, we lived with three German shepherds, two bitches and a younger male. Both of the
bitches would clean the ears and face of the male puppy by
licking him profusely. Even after he became a mature adult,
they continued to treat him as if he were their puppy. He
seemed to thrive on their maternal attentions.

After the older bitch died, we got a young male, and
when the second female died, we got another bitch puppy.
Poor Butch, the only survivor of our original pack, continued
to bring his head over to the new dogs, obviously hoping to
be groomed by them. They, of course, never did it.

I felt bad for Butch because for so many years he had
been the "Baby Prince," nurtured and indulged by the older
females in the pack. Then, all of a sudden and without warning, not understanding why, Butch was treated as if he were
an old fogy, tolerated, respected, but nevermore indulged. I
often noticed him giving the younger dogs what appeared to
be wistful looks, but if that is what they were, the younger
dogs never got the message.

∞ Life isn't fair. It's not meant to be. Making the best of things means facing the inevitable changes that shatter every illusion that somehow we are in control. Don't kick against the goad.

⌂ After Grief

by Ali Moore

S EVERAL YEARS AGO, I was contacted about two English bulldogs in need of help. Their former mom died tragically in an automobile accident, leaving them orphaned.

Paula had adored her dogs. She and Albert, a certified therapy dog, had been together since his puppy days. They visited hospitals and nursing homes together, bringing cheer to patients and residents. Frances' beginnings were unknown. She had come from a local animal shelter and was just happy to be loved.

When Paula died, Albert and Frances were naturally confused and depressed. We offered love and support to help ease them through their grieving period, and once their spirits improved, we began to search for their new homes.

Albert and Frances now live with two wonderful couples. Both have grown children, so the dogs have become their babies and are showered with love. These two formerly companion dogs (and their humans) get together annually for a reunion. Albert has gone on to become a "spokesdog" for a local pet-supply chain, but he devotedly continues his charitable work and has plans to write a book.

I believe that Paula somehow guided us in placing her dogs. We couldn't have found better homes for them! We remain in constant touch with both couples as well as with Paula's sister, Jill. Through Jill, I have realized how very special Paula must have been. I only wish that I had had the pleasure of knowing her myself.

∞ *Dogs grieve as we do, for those we have loved and lost. Recovery from depression depends on the willingness to go on with one's life, making the best of things and doing for others.*

🏠 Governor Baxter

by Gary Stafford

W E WENT TO SEE THIS DOG because a friend of ours said he needed someone to adopt him. Since he was a bird dog and we wanted one for hunting, we would surely like him. When we arrived at the designated log cabin deep in the woods, the dog was nowhere to be found. The present owners weren't concerned, because he never ran very far, they said. The eighteen-month-old German shorthaired pointer had been a gift to them, but he had never bonded with his new owners.

Eventually we found him, took him home, and began the task of rehabilitating and conditioning this loving boy we called Baxter. His obedience training went well. He was quite birdy, but his recalls were a real trial. Once he started to run, there was no stopping him. After several months of patient work and behavior modification, we had Baxter responding at 100 percent. We thought he was a wonderful addition to our family, but two of the older female dogs took a very strong dislike to him. After a couple of serious fights, we decided to find a new home for the "gov'ner." We carefully screened several potential owners, and then we sent Governor Baxter to his new family in New Hampshire, where he still resides. We stay in touch with his new owners, who affirm that Baxter enjoys being part of the family. He goes camping and hiking with them. We miss him and hope that someday we will own another German shorthair.

∞ *Don't give up if first efforts seem to fail. By continuing to try, you will surely succeed in accomplishing your goals. As in the case of Governor Baxter, things often work out in the end.*

🏠 A Dog for Meredith

by Susan Babbitt

A NUMBER OF YEARS AGO, several acquaintances of a family friend decided that she would benefit enormously from the addition of a dog into her life.

Meredith was in her mid-eighties at this time, and one might wonder how she would manage to take care of a new furry companion. How would she adapt to the antics of a lively young dog?

Sam was a small black poodle that had been owned by a family now moving away. They were unable to take the dog along with them to their new home. Reluctantly, they gave him up, and Sam got a new home with our friend Meredith.

Over the years we have continued to be in contact with Meredith and her son. Meredith and Sam have obviously thrived in their relationship. Her son reported that every night his mother, who is now ninety-seven years old, still makes a bed for Sam at the foot of her bed. And every night, just as soon as Sam thinks Meredith is asleep, he climbs off his doggie bed and walks to the head of her bed, leaps up, and joins Meredith under the covers.

∞ *Never underestimate the value of others' advice.*

··

⌂ The Dog That Could Not Swim

by Fred Lanting

D OGS THAT CANNOT SWIM ARE UNHEARD OF by most people, but it was my fate to have bred and trained such an animal. Abbie managed to keep her head above water. She didn't drown, but she wasn't really swimming. She paddled in a completely upright position and since her body was vertical, she could make no real forward progress.

One weekend toward the end of the summer, Abbie earned her Schutzhund title and made a nice showing in the conformation ring, too, both prerequisites for her breed survey. At the end of the day of competing, Abbie and I and a number of other dog-handler teams took advantage of the lake near the testing grounds.

I had brought a bicycle tube and pump along. Abbie needed something like water wings to keep from sinking or remaining vertical. I doubled the tube into a figure-eight, folded it back on itself, and maneuvered it past her legs so it fit around her waist before I inflated it. With Abbie's butyl tutu in place, we headed for the lake. Several wary human females screamed about a dog being attacked in the water by two boa constrictors. "Snakes!" they yelled. "There are snakes on your dog!"

Despite the hysteria, the bicycle tube served two worthy purposes. First, it enabled Abbie to be in a horizontal position so she could swim properly, and second, it gave everybody a good laugh.

∞ *If you can't do it one way, do it another!*

⌂ Passing the Torch

by Yvette Piantadosi-Ward

ONE OF THE PROBLEMS WITH a multiple-dog household is that the females usually come into heat within a week or two of each other. So for close to four months (in my situation, anyway), someone is always in heat. The females do not mind, but our two male dogs have had to learn to ignore these signs.

Last spring, our oldest female came into heat at twelve years of age. The stud male of our household disregarded her season. We attributed his behavior to her age, but we also thought it was because he knows he is not allowed to breed without a command to do so.

On the twenty-seventh day of her season, this venerable lady became the star attraction to a newbie in our pack, an eight-month-old male. He started to show interest in the old girl, but we more or less ignored this behavior. We thought she was no longer fertile, and the vet agreed. The young male gave it a try anyway. The vet said that since the conjugal tie was so short due to her being infertile, we shouldn't worry. So much for science!

Sixty-six days later, our good old girl gave birth to a lone male puppy that turned out to be superb in every way. He is now part of our pack and we watch him closely when a female is brought in for breeding, because he already seems to have a knack for knowing the exact date to breed a female in heat. Or is it just genetic memory?

∞ When things you haven't planned pop up in your life, try to make the best of them, for often, they are blessings in disguise.

··

🏠 Someone's Gotta Go

by Jack Ryan

F ROM THE DAY WE MOVED into our new house, the four boys and I began working on their mother. "Boys should have a dog to care for," I argued. "A puppy will teach them responsibility."

Diane wasn't buying it. "I know who'll get stuck with all the work," she said. We reached a stalemate in the great puppy debate. It was five against one, but Diane had veto power. Then, North Shore Animal League brought an RV filled with puppies to the parking lot of the local pet store. "Let's just take a look," I said. "What can that hurt?" I knew that if we could get a puppy into Mom's hands, the battle would be won.

We came home that morning with a month-old mixed-breed fur ball that we called Jody. We knew nothing about caring for a puppy, and our beautiful new home with its plush wall-to-wall carpet got the worst of it. The boys soon forgot their promise to walk Jody. A month passed, and Diane's patience reached its limit. "I love that puppy," she said, "but the puppy has to go back. End of discussion."

I knew that arguing wouldn't help. The boys were crying, but Diane was right. It was time for desperate measures. Holding

Jody in my lap, I grabbed her right front paw and said, "Wave bye-bye to Mommy." Mom melted, just as she had in the RV at the pet store.

∞ *Sometimes making the best of things means finding another way.*
....

⌂ The Closest He Could Get

by Theresa Mancuso

W HEN I ARRIVED AT THE EMERALD CITY DOJO, eager to watch my nephew and his companions work through a session in aikido, I spied a formidable looking pit bull/Vizsla mix and doggie fever struck.

"This is *my* place," he seemed to say from his position hovering near the mat. I eased my way closer to the dog and addressed him softly and respectfully in a whisper.

"Good boy; that's a fine fellow." Smudge could have cared less.

"This is *my* place."

In front of all those people, I was surely not going to back down. And just as I went fishing in my pockets for a treat of sorts to offer him, the red dog seemed to change his mind about me. Mr. Big Bad Boy, Threatening Mean Pit-Bull Menace suddenly became the doggie in the window, the one with the waggily tail. In an instant, we were wrapped in a friendly embrace as I caressed his soft velvety coat. We stayed that way most of the ninety-minute aikido session. Smudge never moved from my arms or away from his special place. At the end of the session, as each participant left the room-sized rubber mat, he or she made a bow to the portrait of the founder of aikido and to the other martial artists, and then came to Smudge who received each one with licks, wags, and doggie blessings. At my nephew's wedding four days later, Smudge appeared as a guest with the sensei. When Smudge saw me, he responded like a lifelong buddy, wiggling his back end and waving greetings with his tail.

∞ *As they say in aikido, if you meet a potential enemy with peace and respect, it will be a different kind of encounter.*

⌂ Spanky's Favorite Toy

by Marlene Sandler *

T HERE WAS A WOMAN WHO LIVED in the country with a wonderful Labrador called Spanky that loved to play in her old cast-iron bathtub. The woman had placed pillows around the floor so Spanky could get in and out of the bathtub without injury. When they moved from the country house to the city, Spanky became very depressed, and the woman called me for help. They had moved before, so it was quite bewildering.

I asked the woman if she had forgotten to bring along his things when they moved. "No," she responded. "I brought along his stuff—all 5,286 tennis balls, the 5,863 Frisbees, all the old shoes, plushy toys, and squeaky things—everything."

"No," Spanky countered, "you brought all *your* toys—your bed, your bureau—*your* toys—not mine. You didn't bring my bathtub."

So, there they were in a beautiful townhouse with a fiberglass bathtub quite unlike the one they had before. The new bathtub had doors, and Spanky couldn't get in. His favorite toy, the bathtub, had been left behind.

"Sure enough!" she said. "He played there every morning."

I tried to explain to Spanky that they hadn't brought the trees with them from the other place, and being an experienced mover, he understood. Plumbing is like trees, I told him; it can't be taken with you. Spanky would not be comforted. Finally, the woman removed the shower doors and put something comfortable in the new bathtub so he could get in and out, and Spanky became a much happier dog.

∞ *We can help others to make the best of things by taking the time to understand and appreciate their real needs and wishes.*

*Marlene Sandler is a well-known animal communicator. The names in her anecdotes have been changed to protect Marlene's clients' confidentiality.

⌂ The Perfect Pom

by Joan Bolger

MY DOG GINO, a pint-sized Pomeranian with a lion's heart, was determined not to fail in our housebreaking campaign.

I decided one very hot summer night to go to bed a little earlier. I dutifully took Gino outdoors to relieve himself, but he had no need to go. We went back in and went to sleep, both in my bed since Gino used his bed as a toy box. Several hours later, I awakened to hear scurrying footsteps near the bed, the pitter-patter of Pomeranian paws. I also heard the squeak of Gino's toys, the bounce of his ball, the scraping of a bone being dragged. I opened one eye and then the other. I strained my ears. I watched silently as the small fluff of a dog quietly removed every single toy from the dog bed. I was fascinated and wondered what he was doing playing with everything in the middle of the night. Then, when the bed was empty, Gino leaped in and deposited a very sizeable relief package.

With a chuckle, I realized that I had failed to put down newspapers in the usual spot where Gino could relieve himself when I was not at home or if I were asleep. Making the best of a hard situation, my little champion solved the dilemma as perfectly as he could. He used his toy box (that is, his converted bed) as a private bathroom rather than soil the floor.

∞ *Think outside the box.*

⌂ Rain Dog

by Jolanta Benal

I USED TO MELT AWAY FROM CIVILIZATION at the barest hint of falling water. When it rained, I stayed at home if at all possible. But then I got a dog.

Izzy was a yellow prick-eared street dingo with a big heart and energy to burn. Whenever I picked up her leash, Izzy bounced into the air, one, two, three, or four times—perfectly, straight up. She could run for hours. Hot? Cold? Hailstones the size of eggs pounding down from the sky? Izzy didn't care.

When Izzy didn't get enough exercise, she didn't fuss. Instead, she lay on the floor and methodically licked away the varnish down to bare wood. Izzy needed a *good long* run, each and *every* day, and if I didn't like the rain, how did I feel about refinishing my floors? Reluctantly, grudgingly, I started taking Izzy to the park for at least an hour every day.

In pelting rain, Prospect Park is almost empty. Heavy rain thunders down, blocking out the city noise, and on the grayest days, you can barely see the buildings that surround it. Prospect Park becomes a dream of solitude, respite for a woman and her dog. Izzy luxuriates, deep in her unknowable delights.

I'm not amphibian yet, but I don't mind the rain any more. Sometimes I leave the umbrella at home, and that might shock anyone who knew me when . . . except that I have an even deeper confession to make. I . . . well, the truth is, I love the smell of wet dog.

··

⌂ Fashion Defeats Fear

by Paul Sutton

A LOT OF DOGS I KNOW ARE TERRIFIED of loud noises, particularly fireworks. My three Border collies, Whisper, Summer, and Sunny, are no exception. They become extremely agitated and frightened by loud sounds. All they have to hear is the first whoosh as the rockets go up, and they run to me and leap on my lap. That's some feat, with the three of them shaking and panting, but I just have to comfort them.

I know the advice is to ignore them, but could anyone ignore a frightened child? The annoying thing is that the use of fireworks has increased. It isn't only bonfire night we have to prepare for now, but here in the U.K. many other occasions such as birthdays, barbeques, and New Year's Day are all fireworks time.

In fact, during the summer it seems like they go off at least once a month! I have tried all sorts of things to calm down the dogs, like loud music, encouraging them to play, and using Rescue Remedy (homeopathic drops). Then last year, someone told me that putting them in T-shirts might help. So I got out three of my most colorful and fetching Ts and duly put them on, tying them snugly round their waists. I don't know if it's because they feel cuddled in the clingy cotton, but it certainly

---

seemed to help a bit. And the dogs looked so cute too, like a miniature football team. They will definitely be wearing their T-shirts again this year.

∞ *Fashion makes a difference in how you feel.*

🏠 Like 'Em or Not

by Neal C. Jennings

IT IS WELL KNOWN THAT PET VISITS benefit the elderly in health care centers. They help lower patients' blood pressure, calm those who are stressed, and raise the spirits of lonely and depressed seniors. Most pet visits are well received, but as we know, all individuals are not necessarily pet lovers—as the following illustrates.

An evaluation of three new volunteer pet teams got off to a bad start when they stopped at one woman's room. She began to scream loudly, imagining that the large dog at her door was a monster. As the teams moved quickly to the next room, a man reading his paper in the back of the room was asked, "Would you like to see my dog?" He remarked that he could see it quite well from where he was.

Fortunately, the remaining visits were well received. Two poodles, Jacques and Jill, were in a down/stay near the wall in a care center during the orientation of a small group of prospective volunteers. A lady pushing a man in a wheelchair noticed the dogs and picked up Jill, the toy, and placed her on the gentleman's lap. Because the dogs' leashes were tied together, Jacques, a twenty-pound miniature, felt a tug on his leash, leaped into the air, and landed on the man's lap alongside Jill. The poor fellow's comment after the dust settled was, "I really don't like dogs."

∞ *Not everyone can share our enthusiasm about the things we love. To improve relationships, learn to be interested in the things that interest others.*

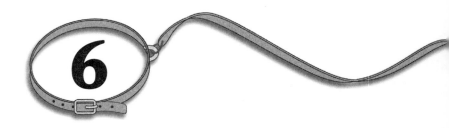

Leashes and Collars:
Work and Play in the Real World

EVERY DOG MUST LEARN TO WEAR a collar and a leash. Our puppies fit themselves into life's expectations, balking at first, perhaps, but gradually learning to do the right thing in the right way.

Humans have collars and leashes of another sort, symbolic, but no less real. We balk at them, too, sometimes, but if we're wise, we know we need to learn how to negotiate the real business of work and play in everyday life. Whatever the game, whatever the job, there's always someone in charge. There's a boss in every situation. It's no use pulling ahead or lunging forward, or dragging behind and refusing to move. The choreography of work and play in the real world is not a matter of choice but of necessity. We must learn the dance if we wish to participate.

Whatever the job might be, the greater our commitment to quality, the greater will be our satisfaction. Work is necessary to earn a living. It pays the rent or mortgage, buys food and clothing, and makes it possible to enjoy some pleasures along the way. Every day, millions of us put on our collars and leashes, so to speak, and go forth to the job. For some people, work poses difficult challenges, burdens that tax the strength. But doing a job the best we can, by putting heart into it, spiritually enriches us.

Working dogs and ordinary pets teach us how to tackle tasks. Many dogs have real jobs in search and rescue or as guide dogs, therapy dogs, seizure alert dogs, bomb sniffers, or police and military canines. Most dogs work at home by loving and guarding family and property. Whatever dogs do, they do it with heart. It works for them; let it work for you!

🏠 You Can't Dog-Proof Everything

by Sara Stopek

I HADN'T BEEN ABLE TO figure out why we were powering through the cat food . . . until this morning, when I found our dog, Emmett, on the dining table, cleaning the cat-food bowls. We feed our kittens on the dining table so they won't annoy the big cats on the counter, which is clearly dog-proof, dog-forbidden, and (when occupied by senior cats) dog-unfriendly.

Emmett clearly wasn't thinking. Appropriate responses might have been "Yikes, caught in the act," or "Sorry, lady, overwhelmed by temptation," or "Please think I'm cute so you're not annoyed." Instead, he looked more like, "Hi!" or maybe, "Hey, look, cat food! Wow!" Emmett just hopped down politely when I asked him to vacate the dining table.

How did we ever get this far without a rule that says, "No dogs on the dining table?"

I guess the matter just never came up. Well, there *was* that time the entire homemade babka disappeared, but he seemed so humbled by that digestive experience. His tableside manners have always been lovely, never a paw on the knee or a chin on the lap.

How long has *this* been going on? He wasn't saying, but it did occur to me that this may be the secret of Emmett's great love for the new cats. There's an interesting side effect. The junior cats can eat on the floor and the dog doesn't muscle (or muzzle) in. I attribute this to tiny feline ferocity, but perhaps

Emmett's learned that good things come to those who wait. What a good boy!

∞ *Mutual cooperation overcomes all boundaries, all inadequacies, all feelings of lack. When you need something, analyze the situation and be ready to make necessary accommodations. Invest yourself in cooperative efforts!*

⌂ Who's the Boss?

by Dr. Nancy Bekaert

I N THE BACK OF MY MINIVAN, I placed a four-by-five-foot wooden platform that I constructed to accommodate my four German shepherd dogs. My alpha dog, however, a scrappy little terrier mutt, claimed the upfront passenger seat for himself and allowed none of the other dogs into the front of the car. Forget about the fact that the shepherds were twice his size or that there were four of them!

At a stoplight one day, the terrier "boss" got up, walked to the back of the van, and stood staring silently at the pack. Three eighty-pound shepherds immediately crawled off the platform, and the fourth moved over to make room.

The boss, not yet happy with this offering, moved over to stare directly into the eyes of the fourth shepherd, who once again moved aside. They continued this game until the fourth shepherd finally got off the platform and gave way to the silent command of his superior.

Finally satisfied with his conquest, the boss returned to the front seat and went back to sleep.

∞ *Accept your place in the scheme of things.*

··

⌂ Pit Bull Mama

by Michael Marino

I F YOU'RE LIKE MANY PEOPLE, you probably think pit bulls are rough, tough, mean dogs, untrustworthy and dangerous. And you'd be dead wrong! Zina, our own little warrior princess, is a six-and-a-half-year-old American pit bull terrier with the best disposition you'd ever hope to see, not only in a dog, but in a person as well. There's no devotion quite like hers when it comes to our grandson, Richie. Just a toddler, Richie easily holds his own when playing with Zina.

Zina watches over our grandson like a loving mother watching over the cradle of her firstborn child. Perhaps, in Zina's eyes, Richie is her child. One day Richie and his cousins, all of whom were less than three years old, were all in a very macho mood. When his two cousins piled on top of Richie in a tackle maneuver that would put the New York Giants to shame, Zina sprang into action. Off to the rescue! With delicate precision, our pit bull mama reached for the kids who perched atop Richie's butt with him flattened on the floor. One by one, Zina gently removed each child—by the seat of the pants!

So much for ferocious pit bulls. Ours is a merciful angel, always on the job.

∞ *Fulfill your obligations when you take on responsibility, don't judge by appearances.*

⌂ My Fierce Little Protector

by Donna Ramsay

O N MY SIXTEENTH BIRTHDAY, my parents gave me a six-week-old female dachshund pup that I named Gretel. Our home was always filled with kids and animals. Gretel soon had the run of the place. None of my friends, parents, and siblings could come near me without her approval. She was my fierce little protector, always there to send me off to school or work and waiting for me when I got home.

As Gretel approached ten years of age, she became very sick and the vet said she would most probably have to be put down. I told the vet that if it was Gretel's time to go, that was okay, but I couldn't bear to see her in pain. Suddenly, she seemed to get better and became her old self again. Over the next few months, my family decided to move west. As we drove the 3,000 miles to Arizona, Gretel sat next to me at full attention.

Within two weeks of our arrival, we rented a home and settled in. The first night there, lying by my side, Gretel passed away. To this day I believe she thought she had to protect me on my way to Arizona. Once we were safely there, her job was done, and she could rest in peace. We buried Gretel in the desert on the side of a mountain, and I know she is still watching over me, my fierce little protector.

∽ *Loyalty and duty make us cling to life until our work is done, and when it is, we may peacefully pass on.*

⌂ The Lion Tamer

by Julie Marlow

I EAGERLY AWAITED the arrival of my first imported fully titled German shepherd dog from the Czech Republic. I knew this dog only from photographs, and I studied key Czech phrases in preparation.

I'm an experienced breeder of working dogs and a veterinary technician of fifteen years, but I was still no match for my new dog, an incredibly strong and fearless animal. After being cooped up for twenty-four hours in air cargo, his eyes didn't shine with reciprocity. To this proud giant I was no friend, but a captor who had removed him from the only life he knew.

Our first game of ball was challenging. I reached to take the ball from him. With huge teeth snapping, he started barking like a police dog stopping a criminal. Frozen stiff, I tried to recall the Czech words for calling off a dog, but I couldn't remember a thing, not even my name. He held me at bay for ten minutes before the right command came to mind. Slowly I rose and put the leash back on. I did eventually get him to drop the ball on command.

These canines are highly trained professionals that won't sell out for American-made dog biscuits. Never stick your head in front of a lion unless you're a lion tamer.

∞ *Getting to know others takes time and patience, especially at the work site, where people are sometimes guarded in their approach to colleagues.*

 The Sting

by Jenny Moir

ANYONE WHO HAS BEEN STUNG by a wasp knows how painful it can be and is probably still very wary of insects to this day. Roddy was no different.

A tan-and-white papillon, Roddy went through a sixteen-week course in advanced sound training from Hearing Dogs for Deaf People. He was taught to respond to everyday household sounds like the doorbell and telephone by touching his trainer to alert her and then leading her to the source of the sound.

Toward the end of his training, Roddy was unfortunately stung by a wasp and had a severe allergic reaction. He collapsed and was rushed to the vet for emergency life-saving treatment. It was touch and go for a while, but Roddy recovered and successfully completed training. Last month he went to live with Doreen Amos.

Not long after he moved in with Doreen, Roddy rushed to her and started scrabbling at her, alerting her that something was going on. Doreen asked, "What is it, Roddy?" He led her immediately to his dog bed, where she saw a wasp buzzing around his bedding. As soon as Doreen disposed of the insect, Roddy happily curled up in his bed and went to sleep.

Although hearing dogs are trained to respond just to sounds, Roddy not only understood that it was a wasp that had hurt him in the past, he used his initiative and hearing-dog training to take care of it.

∞ *Never underestimate the intelligence of another being.*
....

⌂ The Enforcer

by Deborah Palman

S OMETIMES A DOG ENFORCES human rules in a dog pack. Years ago I had an older female who brooked no nonsense from younger pups. She enforced a "no unnecessary noise" rule when she and a male pup were riding in crates side by side in the back of my car.

On one particularly long trip, I was in a hurry. I put their supper into their crates at a rest area before driving on, planning to remove the bowls at the next stop. After finishing his meal, the bored puppy began to play with his metal bowl, banging it about and making a tremendous racket as he bounced it repeatedly against the crate. I was on a busy interstate highway. I couldn't safely stop to remove the bowl, and the sound of it careening off the sides of the crate began to get nerve-wracking after a while.

Nevertheless, I knew that yelling would be quite ineffective and might actually cause the puppy to continue playing loudly just for the attention he would get every time I called back to him. I was finally getting resigned to putting up with the noise when suddenly, my older female exploded with a roar, barking and thrashing about in her own crate to discipline the unruly youngster. Just as suddenly, the noise stopped. I heard the puppy sigh and lay down in his place. Clearly, my alpha female had triumphed. She happily resumed her evening nap, knowing she would not be disturbed.

∞ *Playing by the rules keeps life in order. Show respect for authority.*

⌂ Atlas Finds His True Vocation

by Tracie Karsiens

ALTHOUGH ATLAS EXCELLED in conformation and obedience competition, he lacked a certain joie de vivre that made me wonder what he'd really love to do. One day I realized that Atlas was actually manifesting typical signs of herding instinct in his everyday behavior with cats and other animals. Perhaps herding was what Atlas was meant to do. I found a place where untrained dogs could be tested for herding instinct. I'm a city girl, not very comfortable with sheep or goats. Nevertheless, I signed Atlas up, and off we went!

Atlas was a different dog from the moment he saw sheep. He became incredibly focused and excited. When our turn came, I went with him into the pen, assuming that Atlas needed my presence. Much to my surprise, Atlas could have cared less if I were there or not. He was in absolute heaven. He loved the sheep, loved to work, and loved doing what he was made for. His gait was better than it ever was in the show ring. He was amazing as he worked with boundless joy and enthusiasm written all over him.

Atlas earned the first leg of his Herding Capability Tested (HCT) title that day, and we began herding lessons shortly thereafter. I'm not crazy about herding, but Atlas loves it and I do it for him. There's nothing more satisfying than to see a dog doing what it was bred to do.

∞ *We should all be lucky enough to find the things we were meant to do.*

⌂ Agility Is Fun

by Paul Sutton

FROM THE VERY BEGINNING, my Border collie, Whisper, loved competing in agility—and so did I. Dogs may not enter agility competitions until they are eighteen months old, so it was with excitement and a certain amount of trepidation that we entered our first show when Whisper was just under two years old. Now she's twelve years old, and over the years in her career, Whisper has won more than a hundred rosettes in agility. Sad to say, my little champion is retired now due to arthritis.

These days I compete with Summer and Sunny, Whisper's offspring. Training them was eventful, and Summer's first attempts were nothing short of disastrous. At her first show, Summer did one jump and left the ring. Later, she progressed to doing half a round, then leaping up and biting my bum. It took a year, but she at last started to get some clear rounds.

Sunny was worse. He's taken almost three years, though last year he finally managed his first clear. Sunny is such an unruly dog that his rounds are more like the demolition derby with poles flying in all directions. But he loves agility, too. This year has been the best ever for my Border collie kids, with lots of clear rounds completed.

∞ *True sportsmanship enables us to survive the ups and downs of every mishap as we strive for our own personal best.*

🏠 Beasley's Choice

*by Marlene Sandler**

I WAS AT AN agility course once just to observe the dogs in their competition, hang out, and enjoy the trials. A wonderful German shepherd named Beasley was also there, but he just wasn't doing as well as he normally did in agility events. I knew the trainer was outstanding as an agility handler. Nevertheless, things weren't going well for the trainer or the dog. Although the trainer paid close attention to scenting, fronting, and listening, Beasley the dog just slowed up and refused to go through the paces with his usual vitality.

The concerned trainer could not figure out what was happening. She turned and looked at me, mouthing the words, "What's wrong?"

I listened to Beasley and then responded. "You have a problem in your left hip and because you don't feel well, Beasley won't go any faster. He's afraid you'll get hurt."

The trainer said, "You're right. I do have a problem with my left leg. But why did the other dog I ran through the course do so well?" (It was dog of a different breed.)

I answered, "Because the other dog is young and not so empathetic."

When they got another handler to run Beasley through the agility course, he achieved a perfect score.

∞ *Sometimes when we're trying to get a job done, but we care about others and put their needs first, we might not look so great before the world, and we might not come out on top, but more important values must prevail.*

*Marlene Sandler is a well-known animal communicator. The names in her anecdotes have been changed to protect Marlene's clients' confidentiality.

••

⌂ My Favorite Dog Story

by Louis B. Colby

AFTER OWNING AND BREEDING more American pit bull terriers than any other man in this country, my favorite dog story is of a little old lady named Helen Long. I'm more proud of the dog in this story than of the forty-nine-pound dog I bred who pulled 5,000 pounds on a cart, or of Colby's Dime, a dog so splendid that I get letters more than fifty years after his birth, asking for his descendants. This dog was not nearly so famous—but he really made a difference.

Helen lived in western Massachusetts on a homestead that had been in her family for generations. The home was loaded with antiques and valuables, and she was often the victim of burglars. Someone told her she ought to have a pit bull for protection so she came to me. Now a puppy would not be protection, and certainly she could not handle an aggressive adult dog, but I had just the dog for her, a wonderful pit that "only looked mean" and one she could control.

Word soon got around town that Helen Long had a pit bull, and the robberies stopped. She sent me a note the following Christmas saying that she once again felt safe in her own home.

∞ *The best accomplishments might not always be the most dramatic.*
....

🏠 Princess to the End

by Elli Matlin

I HAD TWO LITTERMATE SISTERS named Bella and Bonnie. Bonnie was the runt. She was so much smaller than the other puppies that we were amazed she even survived. Since we couldn't sell Bonnie, we kept her. We also kept Bella, a dazzling beauty, to be our show puppy. As it turned out, first appearances were deceiving. Bonnie may have gotten a late start, but eventually she got so big she was oversized for the show ring. I made her my obedience dog and showed her in AKC trials.

When we bred Bella, she acted professionally pregnant from the day of breeding to the day of whelping. She crawled into the whelping box and stayed there, content to let the rest of the world go by. Bella was an easy whelper, but she was too much of a princess to be a good mother. She made a weak show of nursing her puppies, leaving the box without finishing the task. Bonnie would hop in, clean the pups, and sleep with them, doing all the real mothering. She even let them nurse on her although she had no milk. Bonnie kept the puppies content until Bella returned to feed them. Bella, Bonnie, and the puppies stayed in the box together until Bella finished nursing and left. Immediately, Bonnie took over, cleaning and licking the babies. Thanks to Bonnie's being an excellent mother, Bella's litters grew up fine. When Bonnie had her own pups, Bella wouldn't even go into the same room with them but remained a princess to the end.

∞ *Do the right thing regardless of who gets the credit for it.*

⌂ Responsible Dog Ownership

by Lonnie Olson

A S THE DIRECTOR OF Dog Scouts of America, I was asked by the local newspaper to come out for a photo of me with the dogs receiving a donation check from a major department store chain.

While waiting in the hall of the local middle school for the photographer, a lady approached who admired the well-behaved dogs, sitting there so patiently waiting. She carefully observed the dogs for a little while and then walked away. She returned after a few minutes and watched them again. They had not moved from their obedient sit position. She had a puzzled look when she asked me about them. I explained that Dog Scouts of America stressed the importance of responsible dog ownership.

She nodded, gazed back down at the obediently waiting canines at my feet, and in all seriousness remarked, "I wish I could get a responsible dog!"

I laughed, but it's really not funny. Do people really think that the responsibility goes with the dog and not the owner? The woman admired the well-behaved dogs, but it wasn't as she thought—the pups didn't come like that. It took a responsible owner to create what she perceived as a "responsible dog."

∞ *It always seems so easy when we see the final product, but the process is where it really happens. All work is about process as well as product. Appreciate every step that leads to the top of the mountain.*
....

⌂ They Keep You Humble

by Mary Frenzel-Berra

ONCE UPON A TIME, I used to feel smug whenever a dog I trained received an obedience title. Eventually, though, it was my fate to attempt to show a dog that refused to sit or down as long as we were out in the sun. She waited until we were nicely settled and then trotted over and planted herself underneath the judges' table. One judge told me, "She'll never pass, but she's the smartest dog in this ring." I could tell that he admired her. She did pass—finally—when I drove her over four hundred miles to an indoor show with air-conditioning.

Another dog of mine once jumped the ring fence and flushed a covey of quail pretty far out. It took me over twenty minutes to retrieve him while the exhibitors patiently waited for us to reappear. Through hard work, that particular dog became nationally ranked, and yes, we did show outdoors again—just not in certain places during hunting season.

Titles, ribbons, and silverware don't matter. If you're in it for the glory, forget about it. The dogs themselves teach us soon enough that embarrassment can evolve into fun, and a sense of self can disappear so humiliation isn't even an issue. It's all about loving dogs, year after year and dog after dog.

∞ *When we set ego aside, our best efforts reap the best rewards.*

⌂ Dog Brothers

by Marlene Sandler*

I KNEW A WOMAN who was very competitive in showing dogs. She had two collies that were brothers and fast friends. One of them, three-year-old Perry, was outstanding, spectacular, a terrific show dog. The other collie, five-year-old Chip, was lovable, terrific, and passable, an okay dog, but not the Westminster kind. The woman always took both dogs to shows together.

Eventually, her fortunes took a downturn, and she could only keep one dog. Painfully, she decided to keep Perry. Chip went to live with another family in a different state. Suddenly,

Perry was no longer such a superstar in the show ring. We were never sure whether old Chip used to coach his younger brother, Perry—or whether his loving presence simply motivated Perry to do the ring exercises correctly. But Chip was most certainly the key. Upon consideration, the woman asked Chip's new family to take Perry in before every show so that he could be around Chip before competing.

As soon as this arrangement was put into place, Perry went back to achieving great scores in agility. Eventually, when the woman's situation improved, the new family was willing to give Chip back to her so both of the dog-brothers were back together again for good.

∞ *Things of the heart affect professional performance. Take care first of that which matters most, and all the rest will follow.*

*Marlene Sandler is a well-known animal communicator. The names in her anecdotes have been changed to protect Marlene's clients' confidentiality.

♠ Dog Leash Ballet

by Joan Antelman

A S A VOLUNTEER DOG WALKER for a Manhattan rescue kennel, I love walking my two charges, Mickey and Sage. Mickey is a ten-year-old husky mix, and Sage is a five-year-old Border collie, both large dogs with distinct personalities and plenty of energy. Every few feet or so during our walk the dogs change sides, requiring me to turn in circles constantly, untangling their leashes. Sometimes, Mickey stops while Sage keeps walking, so I have to extend my arms like a huge, confused bird to give each of them ample freedom of movement.

Eventually, I learned to switch hands the way an experienced juggler would, tossing one leash and then the other to the opposite hand, or moving one after another behind my back, tricky business for a beginning dog-walker. Gradually, I learned to juggle the lead and grew content with my skills in the dog leash ballet. Often, I don't know whose leash I have in which hand, but finally we reach the dog run, where the leashes are unclipped and the dogs set free to play.

Once there, Mickey desires another drink of water, while Sage wants to catch the ball and hold it in his mouth rather than continuing to chase it. Eventually, we amble back to the kennel and up the stairs, where I say my good-byes. The dog leash ballet is over for another day. There will be more dancing to come the following morning, and I can't wait!

∞ *The little aggravations in work and play can be part of what makes it fun. Dogs must learn leash requirements, and so must we as we accept the rules and regulations that harness us at work and play, ties that bind us to the common cause rather than our own personal whims.*

🏠 A True Gentleman

by Theresa Mancuso

WHEN MY DOG GRIP was ten months old, he was already a formidable giant of ninety-six pounds, all muscle and energy, with a head as big as a basketball. Grip's mild manner won friends everywhere we went, but on some occasions, Grip's working dog character emerged. He was a powerful companion with strong protective instincts.

On my daily walks through Prospect Park, I had met an Italian gentleman, Willie, who took a fancy to my German shepherds. We often walked together in the Great Meadow with other dog friends and their pets. One day I arrived home from grocery shopping to find Willie waiting for me on the front porch. He offered to help me carry the groceries upstairs. We shared a cup of coffee while he spoke about his apple orchards in northern Italy. When it was time for him to go, he made amorous advances that I didn't appreciate. As he put his arms around me and drew me closer, trying to kiss me, I said firmly and loudly, "No, Willie, don't."

Immediately, my gentleman Grip raced from the far end of my apartment and leaped up between Willie and me, pushing him away from me and holding him at bay with two large paws planted squarely on each shoulder. He didn't bite or injure Willie, but separated us, reinforcing my refusal. As quickly as he could, my guest left my apartment and I never saw him again.

⌂ Meenie's Christmas Party

by Gail Smart

MEENIE IS A BRINDLE BOXER whose full tail is still not approved in English show circles. As a puppy, she developed a complex, being last in every competition and becoming stressed and anxious at shows. We stopped doing open shows but continued with fun shows and club events.

It was time for the Christmas party, and this year Meenie would go alone because Ugly, my other boxer, was feeling poorly. I wondered if Meenie could cope without him or if we'd have to leave the party early.

We formed teams for the party games and started with the sausage race, in which each dog is supposed to retrieve a sausage from the pile and bring it back. Meenie dived into the pile with great enthusiasm and ate as many as possible before deigning to obey the recall.

The balloon race was next. We had to individually pick up and inflate a balloon while balancing a toy on our heads. Getting the hang of these races, Meenie leaped into the finished balloons and dispersed them round the room.

Then we had the hula-hoop race. Filled with party spirit, Meenie and I tried to get through the hoop together, but alas, only Meenie is slim. The ball we were dribbling at the time disappeared completely from our view.

At the end of the evening, Meenie won the prize for being the dog that enjoyed the party most. Meenie hasn't been stressed out since; she never knew what fun shows could be!

∞ *Having fun is the best way to overcome self-consciousness and other negative feelings that cause stress and anxiety. Put yourself into the action, and you'll increase the fun and decrease the stress.*

....

⌂ The Nose Knows: Advanced Search

by Henry C. Hicks

I RECEIVED A CALL at the beginning of my shift one evening to assist the narcotics unit in searching a suspect's vehicles. Ankera, my Belgian Malinois police dog and partner, and I made our way to the parking lot, and I presented two of the suspect's vehicles to my partner.

Ankera showed no interest in either vehicle, so we started back up to the apartment. When Ankera and I reached the door of the apartment, it opened, and one of the detectives started coming out of the apartment with a bag of evidence.

I started to tell him that Ankera didn't show any interest in the cars, but as soon as he stepped out of the doorway, Ankera pulled hard on her leash. I thought she was after the coffee table where the detectives had found half a kilo of dope, but I let her continue into the room.

Ankera walked past the table and continued into the kitchen, going directly to the electric stove. Ankera then sniffed very hard along the top edge of the stove and sat down, which is her alert to tell me that she has found the odor of narcotics. The detectives said they had checked the stove. I lifted the top anyway and revealed the burners. Two kilograms of powder cocaine were hidden between them.

∞ *When in doubt, bring in an expert to make sure the job is done well.*
················

⌂ Who Moved My Kong?

by Jackie E. Athey

WHEN TESS WAS ALIVE, she ruled the boys with an iron paw—forget the velvet glove. She always had to have whatever toy the boys were playing with. Well, the only toys allowed outside are balls and Kongs, and the Kongs are the paws-down favorite.

When I was outside, Tess didn't let the boys play Kong with me; she had to be the only one. After so much chasing, she would always bring the Kong halfway back, then put it on the ground and stand over it keeping it between her front paws.

Sioleiligh would sneak up behind her, drop to the ground, and crawl between her front and back paws far enough for him to reach the Kong. While Tess looked at me, Sioleiligh grabbed the Kong, snuck out from under her, turned, and dashed away. About the time he turned to run, Tess would suddenly realize that something was amiss. She'd look for the Kong, but horrors! It was gone. She'd search frantically, and then she'd see Sioleiligh holding the Kong with a smirk on his doggie face. The chase was on! Tess never failed to retrieve the Kong, but it was a good chase all over the yard, and Sioleiligh always looked pleased with himself afterward.

∞ *It's the challenge that allures. Satisfaction isn't necessarily about winning, but more about being in the game.*

⌂ Willy's Promotion

by Anthony Jerone

WILLY WAS A two-year-old German shepherd tunnel dog that worked with the United States Army in Vietnam. Trained to sniff out concealed tunnels that were invisible to the naked eye, he would sit and wait to indicate he had found a tunnel or an enemy presence. The enemy knew how valuable dogs like Willy were. The Viet Cong would pay twice as much for Willy's ear—enough for a Vietnamese farmer to buy ten water buffalo—as they would for my shoulder patch.

On this particular day, I called the infantry behind me to say my dog had indicated either a concealed tunnel or a booby trap. As we approached Willy to check it out, a Vietnamese woman jumped out of the hole with two grenades. The pins were out, and she was ready to throw them. There were two bodyguards assigned to me, one on my left and another on my right. As she jumped out of the hole, they fired at her, and she fell back in, taking the grenades down with her. Among the dead, Willy found one of the top ten Viet Cong, wanted by the U.S. military for setting booby traps that killed our soldiers on the Ho Chi Minh Trail.

Willy was accredited with finding that individual, and there was a ceremony back at base camp to promote Willy from the rank of private first class to corporal, with the brigadier general coming down to present us with the citation.

∞ *Good training and true dedication will always be rewarded.*

⌂ The Value of Better Planning

by Bev McQuain

BACK IN THE DAYS when I used to sell dogs, a customer once expressed concern that his patrol dog was so friendly he might not protect him in an emergency.

In order to test the true responses of a trained patrol dog, one must catch both dog and handler completely by surprise.

A few weeks later, I parked out of sight, quieted my three personal dogs, and watched the path where I knew he took his dog for a nightly walk. When I spotted the pair in the distance, I got out of my station wagon and hid behind a bush. When they came by, I flew out of the dark and jumped on the back of the owner. The impact took him to the ground.

The dog responded exactly as he should have. He grabbed my upper arm, dragged me off, and continued to attack until the handler realized that it was me, and called off the dog.

Accepting the owner's grateful thanks, I returned to my car. There I found the wagon's interior completely destroyed: door upholstery clawed off, bites ripped out of the foam-packed dashboard, steering wheel broken, door handle missing in action. My dogs had seen me fighting with a human and a dog. I had protective clothing, but I left my vehicle defenseless against dogs desperately trying to escape to save their master.

∞ *When planning, try to account for all details—but keep in mind that the best laid plans of mice and men . . .*

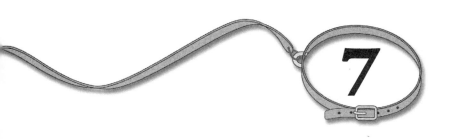

Wag That Tail:
Cultivate Your Sense of Humor

ONE OF GOD'S GREATEST GIFTS is a good sense of humor. When we have learned to laugh at ourselves as well as the million-and-one other crazies all around us, we will have found the touchstone of a joyful heart. Laughter is a blessing no one can deny you.

Laughter arises from insight into the human condition, such as it is, and acceptance that this earthly journey is full of incongruities and surprises. That's what makes it funny.

My dog Geisty had the best sense of humor I've ever seen in a dog. With her great heart, Geisty never lost her interminable doggie smile. One of her favorite jokes was one she played on a small terrier who lived down the hall from us. Whenever we passed his door, she would sniff along the bottom of the door as we waited for the elevator right across the narrow corridor. The terrier, on picking up her scent, would launch into a roar of yelps and barks announcing the "almost intruder." Geisty would turn and look at Grip and they'd break out into the biggest doggie smiles you have ever seen.

In all of life's solemnity, there are moments of mirth woven into the fabric of human experience. If we but open up our eyes to the wonderment of reality as it unfolds around us and within us, we can learn to appreciate the jovial and sometimes ridiculous nature of ourselves and the rest of the world, too. Laughter is the purest enjoyment we will ever know in this world that poets have called a "vale of tears." Even when I'm crying, I have often been interrupted by my own sense of humor as something incongruously ridiculous presents itself to the mind. I cultivate this art because it keeps me sane, or relatively so.

⌂ Flasher on Board

by Pat Hill

S AXON, A MALE BLACK LAB, was my fourth guide dog and quite a gentleman. He had short, close-cut fur and a compact build, weighing in at sixty-five pounds soaking wet. I have often been told that Saxon was a very alert dog because of the curious expression on his face. When we rode the train, Saxon would lie on the floor under my seat, and as the train pulled into our station, he'd get up and get ready to lead me out. I usually sit close to the driver's spot.

One night we had gone through three of our eleven stops when a man got on the train and sat right across from us. Saxon stood up and jumped onto the seat behind me with his chin digging into my left shoulder.

I heard other passengers move to another part of the train and then someone came and sat next to me. He whispered "Flasher." I reached over and knocked on the door of the driver's compartment. The driver just said "Okay." I heard him radio for assistance. He left the door open between his compartment and the rest of the train. At the next stop, two police officers boarded the train and invited the man to come with them. As the man stood up, they wrapped a blanket around him, and led him off the train. Saxon returned to the floor as if nothing had ever happened.

Sax is retired now and lives with me as a pet. He is twelve years young.

∞ *When necessary, be alert to threats—but relax well in between.*

⌂ Field Training

by Lonnie Olson

O NE DAY, I was out in the field training my golden retriever with four friends and their retrievers. One of their nephews also came along to watch us work our dogs. We were all climbing up a very steep hill, crawling on all fours, when I noticed that I was bringing my right leg (which is artificial) forward each time but not getting any purchase on the terrain. Lo and behold, my prosthesis had snapped right in two at mid-calf and was flopping around inside my knee-high boot like limp spaghetti.

I gasped in surprise and said, "Oh, my God! My leg's broken!"

My husband, Harry, and friend Doug helped me to the top of the hill.

I exclaimed, "Oh, man, it's broken clean in two! We're going to have to amputate!" I unzipped my boot and found that the leg was hanging by a tiny shred of fiberglass "skin."

Harry said, "You're right, it's got to come off," as he pulled out his hunting knife. He quickly slashed the thread of fiber-glass and my leg, with boot still on, fell to the ground with a thud. Then again, that might have been the thud of my friend's nephew passing out. One of the dogs grabbed the amputated leg and ran off with it. We roared with laughter, never stopping to think about the poor kid who didn't know I wore an artifi-cial leg. I wish I could have seen the look on his face before he turned green!

∽ *Learning to laugh at yourself is the best part of humor.*

⌂ Trevor Takes Over

by Anne Martindale

LIFE WASN'T MUCH FUN at the time when I was selecting my first dog. So the first criterion would be its ability to make me laugh. Got myself an Airedale. Got my money's worth. These guys even look funny! People often say, "He doesn't look real. He's like a big stuffed animal." True, but these fascinated viewers haven't experienced Trevor having the crazies. Seventy pounds of projectile terrier can get pretty wild.

Don't visit here unless you've got a sense of humor. Trevor will do his "Let's Play" routine: grab a toy, then a growl, snort, shake, shimmy, and nudge for attention. If you don't chase him, he'll gladly chase you. Washing dishes guarantees a squeaky toy planted plum center of the butt. If that toy doesn't move you, Trevor will systematically try every toy in the house. Prudes need not apply.

We've got sound effects. How about accompanying a yawn with a throaty "whoooooooa"? The raucous snorting of wild boars? Grunts of gleeful satisfaction when ears are getting scratched by self or humans? A whimper of total piteous dejection when a toy is discovered just beyond reach!

Trevor comes driving frequently, so he can hang over the back seat of my station wagon and grin through the back window at cars behind us. People in passing cars point and laugh at his bearded and fuzzy grinning face. The way I see it, giving a human a laugh is a doggone public service.

∞ *Spread mirth however you can.*

⌂ Burying Poppie

by Theresa Mancuso

MY DOG ABBY had been at his bedside with me the night before my dad died at ninety-one. When I knelt at the foot of his bed massaging his feet with holy oil, I had felt the coldness of death beginning to reach through his body. The next morning he died. We gathered round him, my sister, my nieces, and my dog, together singing the songs my father loved, songs he had sung to us in our infancy and childhood, songs we had sung together in the family automobile taking long rides through the countryside when all of us were kids and Poppie was young.

On the morning of his funeral, I joined my nephews as a pallbearer, proud to walk beneath his coffin, helping to carry his cherished remains to the burial site. My dog Abby, ever faithful and much loved by my father, walked tall at my side while we bore him to his final resting place. At graveside, my priest brother incensed the opened earth and sprinkled holy water on the coffin while chanting the final prayers. My heart felt torn from my chest, but at the same time, looking down at my dad's casket, I could see my dog's face peripherally and I had to smile. Dad himself would have chuckled. It seemed to me that Abby might be remembering my dog Grip and his ability to excavate enormous holes. Abby had a look of amazement about her, as if she were thinking, "Holy cow, Grip, you should see this hole for hiding bones!"

∞ *Even in life's tragic hours, there are often moments that salvage a bit of comfort for our hearts, bits and pieces of humor or remembrance that make us stronger for the days to come.*

··

🏠 Doggie Jail

by Elli Matlin

WHEN I WENT TO VISIT my brother in upstate New York, CB had to spend the night in the van. My sister-in-law is not a dog person.

It was a hot summer evening. CB was crated in the van with the van door and the garage door open so that she could get sufficient air and even a breeze, perhaps. When I came out in the morning, CB was gone.

I drove up and down the roads looking for her and calling her name. The farm family across the road reported that she had dropped by for breakfast and then went off with their dogs to swim in the pond. Another neighbor said that CB had eaten breakfast with them, too, before heading up the road.

My brother called the local sheriff. Animal control had picked CB up when she was reported trespassing in a woman's swimming pool. CB was peacefully sleeping in the back of the animal control's pickup truck. She had not yet been brought into the shelter, because she was so wet and smelly from the scummy pond. I went to bail CB out of "Doggy Jail." Fortunately I had her rabies vaccination certificate and she was micro-chipped.

I found her sleeping peacefully in the back of the pickup. She gave me the most disgusted look as if to say, "What took you so long?"

∞ *When it's over, you can often laugh about it. Try laughing sooner. It'll be good for your blood pressure.*

....

⌂ The Cost of Curiosity

by Sandi Davis

SOMETIMES, DOGS CAN be as curious and irrepressible as the most gossipy and intrusive neighbors. There's a price to be paid for curiosity out of control!

The first service dog I ever had was a Samoyed named Darla. The biggest issue I had with her was her curiosity. I had no idea how to keep her nose out of places where it didn't belong. Darla had a mind of her own when it came to investigating. She was irrepressibly curious about things most dogs don't bother with at all. Darla had to know!

One morning I was in the shower when I heard a weird thumping sound and banging in my kitchen. When I checked it out, I found Darla at her nosiest and noisiest. I had set an empty soda case on the floor by my garbage can, ready to be thrown out, but Darla got there first. Darla was curious about it, put her nose into it, and then realized that her head was stuck in the case. This must have distressed her enormously. Off she went, running into the wall, plunging headfirst into cupboards, and banging on anything else she could find trying to get it off of her. I took the offending soda case off her head, and she never put her head in a box again.

∞ *Don't put your nose where it doesn't belong.*
....

⌂ Water Dogs

by Elli Matlin

WHILE GERMAN SHEPHERDS are not known as water dogs, it seems to run in the lines I breed. I'd put my dogs up against any retriever for water sports, and except for the difference in size, I'd even put them up against any Newfoundland for water rescue.

Years ago, we gave a puppy to a cousin of mine for a graduation present. His family, who lived on a lake in New Jersey, always remarked how that pup loved to swim. The only problem was that if the kids were in the water, she'd jump off the deck, grab them by their bathing suits, and drag them back to land. Eventually, she had to be crated whenever the children went swimming.

Now, CB, our champion of all swimmers, was well known as a great water dog. When my friend Rick wanted to teach his dog Canto to swim, we took the two of them to Lake Ronkonkoma and threw the ball. CB would swim out to get it, and Canto, not wanting to lose his ball, followed her into the water. Canto learned to swim thanks to CB.

Another friend of mine had a litter of puppies and purchased a kiddie pool to keep them cool in the summer heat, but the puppies wouldn't go into the water. CB to the rescue! She jumped right in and lay down in the water. The puppies, wanting to play with her, climbed over the edge of the pool and learned to splash around and enjoy the pool.

∞ *Teach by example wherever possible.*

⌂ A Case of Mistaken Identity

by Mary Rodgers

B ACK IN THE DAYS before ordinary folks spayed and neutered their pets, I had Killer, a small red dog, part Pekinese, part spaniel, with remaining parts unknown. Killer had been dumped at the airport, and when a new airport manager didn't want dogs around, I took him home. One day when I got home from work, Killer wasn't there. I telephoned the animal control center, and they said Killer was in the pound.

A boxer bitch had been seen walking the streets, and every male dog in town was right behind her. The shelter staff suggested that I come and pick up Killer the next morning. I went and looked for him in a huge fenced area filled with dogs, but Killer wasn't there.

"Where's Killer?" I asked.

"Oh," the attendant replied, "the females are all in another cage."

The boxer bitch was sitting down when I got to the females' cage. Killer came right to the cage door, looking pleased to see me. He appeared very tired and had a sort of smirk on his face.

"But Killer is a male," I protested. The two attendants looked at each other. They looked at Killer. They looked at the boxer bitch. Then they looked at me. "Oh, oh!" they said.

Killer was asleep before I put him in the car and even slept standing in the bathtub while I washed him. He woke up the next morning still wearing a smile on his face. I never knew what happened to that boxer bitch, but I imagine that out there someplace there are some Pekinese-boxer-spaniel puppies.

ᙄ *Sometimes you can profit by the mistakes of others.*

 Payback Time

by Theresa Mancuso

A UNT MARY WAS DAD'S ONLY SISTER. We loved to visit our childless auntie, who spread out a splendid array of goodies and doted on us.

But, alas, there was Tiny, a very small Chihuahua with great lungs. Tiny could roar; he really could. As a youngster of seven or eight years, I was frightened by the scampering brown beast that came screeching toward me with menacing sharp little teeth. Tiny was a jealous dog. Neither my three brothers nor I would ever have attempted to take his place on Aunt Mary's lap, but Tiny wasn't taking any chances, so he barked at us and tried to nip our heels and ankles. Aunt Mary would say, "It's okay, kids. Tiny won't hurt you."

Fifty years later, I made sure to visit Aunt Mary on all my trips to Utica, and I always brought along my three enormous German shepherds. Their size alone could easily intimidate most mortals, but Aunt Mary, miniature person that she was, had a great heart for dogs. On my first trip to visit her with Grip, Cara Mia, and Geisty, I laughed and said, "Ah, Aunt Mary, remember how Tiny used to scare me! It's payback time." But Aunt Mary only laughed and reached out to pet my dogs as she welcomed them with three big bowls of spaghetti and meatballs slathered with sauce. She put the dishes down on the floor and the dogs dove in hungrily. Aunt Mary grinned at me. "You were saying?" she asked.

∞ *Laugh at what you fear and face it without flinching. Most of our fears come from our own mistaken assessment of reality.*

⌂ Tonto's Favorite Fruit

by Pat Hill

M Y GUIDE DOG TONTO was a male chocolate Lab, long and tall of body, with hazel-colored eyes and a light-brown coat with natural blonde and red highlights. He was quite a beautiful dog.

On a hot summer afternoon, I took Tonto out for a walk. When we returned home, I took him to a grassy area where he could relieve himself.

Tonto proceeded to do his circles, turning himself around and around, so I knew he was about to go. From the sound of it, I thought he might have had loose stools. Then, I heard a man behind me laughing. The man asked me if I knew what my dog was doing.

I tried to remain calm, polite, and dignified. I said, "Why, yes, he's taking a dump."

Before I could say anything further, the man cut me off and said, "No, no, that's not what I mean. Your dog isn't just taking a dump, he's eating the berries off the bush as he goes."

∞ *Avail yourself of good opportunities when they come your way. Never let your chances pass you by.*

⌂ A Walk on the Grass

by Donna Eckenrode

ONE LATE AFTERNOON as my family and I were going through the garage on our way into the house, our German shepherd, Bear, recognized an opportunity to escape. Now, when our luck holds, Bear dutifully follows the crowd into the house without incident. But when Lady Luck smiles on Bear instead, he's rewarded with the wind in his fur as he flies forth, out of the garage and into the world. Being fleet of foot and sharp of nose, he wholeheartedly welcomes a plethora of wonderful smells and exciting adventures as they, too, welcome him.

Although I did not wish to interfere with his joy on this particular occasion, I set out to recapture his attention before he could get too far away. After several futile attempts, we had reached the end of the block, and I saw another opportunity to close in on my runaway dog.

Bear's interest had been captured by something in a neighbor's yard. I tried to sneak up on him, advancing quietly, hoping that the marvel he was examining wouldn't satisfy his curiosity before I could reach him. Then, just when I grabbed hold of his collar, the neighbor's sprinkler system engaged and both of us were drenched. My feelings of stupidity and embarrassment, standing there soaking wet and hoping that no one was watching, was usurped only by Bear's great pleasure at being able to play in the water.

∞ *Take time to smell the flowers—or walk on the lawn. Having fun is sometimes worth the embarrassment.*

⌂ Duke Is Killing Santa Claus

by Donna Ramsay

I WAS ABOUT FIVE YEARS OLD. Duke was our family dog, comparable to the cartoon mutt known as Marmaduke. Known throughout the neighborhood as a lovable, protective, mischievous dog, he made everyone smile as he bounded across the yard, chasing kids, stealing laundry from the neighbor's clotheslines, and just having fun. Above all else, Duke loved my father and would knock him off his feet and play with him when he got home every night.

Late one December evening before Christmas, about fifteen of us children gathered at a neighbor's home with promises that Santa Claus was on his way to spend the evening with us. As we eagerly watched out the window in anticipation of meeting the jolly one, we spotted him. But our joy turned to horror when we witnessed Duke appear out of nowhere and pounce on Santa, knocking him to the ground, tearing at his clothes and beard. We screamed in horror that Duke was killing Santa. My mother rushed out of the house to Santa's rescue. As we sat in tears, Santa appeared, with Duke nowhere in sight. Santa assured us that he was okay, and that Duke just wanted to play. We calmed down, forgetting Duke's attack and went on to have a wondrous, magical night.

Many years later I learned that Duke knew Santa. He was my father, and in Duke's excitement at seeing Dad, he just did what he loved to do—knock Dad off his feet and play.

⌂ Never Let the Dog on the Bed

by Theresa Mancuso

DOGS AT THE MONASTERY did not use human furniture. They were not permitted to climb up on chairs or sleep on beds but instead had their own places, in crates and on the floor. But when I "graduated from monk school" and took up residence on my own in Brooklyn, I knew how I wanted to live.

My dogs and cats thrive on perching wherever their little hearts desire. When I leave my automobile, for example, a doggie driver always ensconces him- or herself in the driver's seat. Dog trainers everywhere seem to say, "Never let the dog on the bed. Something terrible must happen when dogs are allowed to sleep on the bed." And yet, and yet . . .

When Abby was a puppy, she was very small and my other two dogs were almost ninety-pounders. It seemed the wisest plan to crate her, but then, her howls would wake the neighbors and that might mean a dance or two with the co-op board. Instead, I put her on the bed, and that's where she's slept for the past seven years. It works out just fine. Abby never questions my authority, and I never question hers!

Recently, I was discussing this never-let-the-dog-on-the-bed-thing with a friend of mine who is a therapist by profession. She told me that several clients of hers had recently broken up with their lovers and in each case, bar none, the weeping client said, "I'd rather sleep with my dog." My case rests.

∞ *When you feel right about something, don't let fear and intimidation make you doubt yourself. On the other hand, never cling tenaciously to false principles. How does that leave us?*

⌂ A Guide Dog That Was a Thief

by Pat Hill

ONE OF MY GUIDE DOGS was a male black Labrador named Evan, blocky-headed, stocky, long, and tall. He had straight hair. Evan was famous for his antics. He could be so deadpan serious and in a split second do something totally unexpected and hilarious.

On one occasion, when we were walking down the subway platform, I could hear people snickering and laughing. A man asked me if I knew what my dog was carrying, so I checked to find out about it. Several dollar bills were hanging out of his mouth. I knew exactly where he had gotten the money. Evan had stolen it, right out of a street musician's guitar case down the block.

About two weeks later, I was traveling down the same platform when I heard a "Clink, clink, clink!" sort of sound. I stopped, and the sound stopped. I walked, and the sound resumed. What could it be?

Pondering the noise and curious about it, I stopped a second time and checked Evan's mouth. This time, my guide dog was carrying a small basket by the handle—the money collected by that same street musician Evan had stolen from two weeks earlier.

∞ *Bad habits grow quickly.*

....

🏠 Loving Life

by Henry C. Hicks

E ACH YEAR, MY K-9 PARTNER and I get recertified as a team through the United States Police Canine Association. The certification takes place out of state and requires us to pack our bags, drive for several hours, and stay in a motel.

My K9 partner, Ankera, loves this "vacation" each year. She sees it as a chance to sleep in a bed and enjoy being with me twenty-four hours a day for the better part of a week. A couple of years ago, I brought a new handler with me to observe how the certification process worked.

One night, we decided to go out and grab a bite to eat. I left my K9 partner in the room instead of putting her into my police cruiser. We were gone for about thirty minutes, and when we returned, we could hear that the television was on. I thought to myself, "You should have put your dog in the car. This room is probably destroyed!"

As I opened the door, expecting the worse, I found my K9 partner, Ankera, lying on the bed. Almost asleep, she was watching television. She must have stepped on the remote while walking across the bed. What program was she watching? *Cops,* of course.

∞ *Expecting the worst might lead to a funny surprise.*

⌂ "Canine" Saturday Night Fever (or Dancing with My Dog)

by Lori Sash-Gail

M Y MOM, a former Las Vegas show dancer, was buried alive with her magician partner, The Amazing Randel, in California. The next year, quite alive, she married him at Houdini's Castle. Although I was somersaulted in the womb by my acrobatic parents, I thought of myself as straight, narrow, and unscrambled. I own a home, am married to Mr. Conservative, and believe in insurance.

Yet today, as I rinse the flea shampoo from my own dance partner's white hair and clip her eighteen nails in preparation for rehearsal, I realize I'm not so normal. My partner is Shiana, a twelve-and-a-half-year-old West Highland white. We perform together in a modern dance concert. Like Mom and Dad, my feet are planted firmly in the air after all.

The dance piece, set to up-beat music, blends two disciplines: dog training and dance. My part is created out of obedience hand signals for heel, sit, and come. Shiana responds as we move and spin together. There are nineteen different commands, including "Zig zag" (leg weaves), where Shiana weaves through my legs as I walk. My favorite part is Shiana's cue to dance with me. I crouch down and put my chin on the ground with my rear up in a puppy playful bow. Shiana takes the invitation, walks over to me, lies down, and drops her chin to the ground. We face each other, eye to eye, and start to dance.

∞ *What's bred in the bone may come out in the fur.*

⌂ Heidi at the Concert

by Peter Altschul

O NE LAZY SUMMER DAY, my guide dog, a Weimaraner named Heidi, and I attended a concert connected with the Aspen Music Festival. The first half featured a piece by Mahler, a composer I like, and it was a treat. The second half featured a Bruckner symphony, which I found unusually boring.

My faithful canine companion seemed to share my view of the piece, which she demonstrated by sitting up, grunting, and shaking herself. I'm sure dogs prefer some musical styles over others, but I seriously doubt that a Weimaraner can distinguish between Bruckner and Mahler, who were contemporaries. Instead, I suspect that my impatience and disgust communicated itself and that Heidi picked up on it.

She finally consented to lie down quietly, and I resignedly sat back to endure the balance of the work. My reverie, though, was interrupted when I heard a loud slap and felt Heidi's head jerk back.

The person sitting next to me nudged me and whispered, "Do you want to know what your dog was doing?"

"I guess so," I responded cautiously.

"Your dog," she quietly intoned, "was assiduously sniffing the behind of the person sitting in front of you."

∞ *If you're bored, find ways to amuse yourself—but be careful that those things will not annoy someone else.*

⌂ Teaching Tara to Come

by Anthony Jerone

TARA THE TERROR was a German shepherd. She was always busting my chops, but I loved training her. I was doing dog training as a hobby in those days because I wanted to impress people with my skills from the military. I pretty much knew how to get a dog to do exactly what I wanted.

I was teaching Tara the "Come" command. When a training dog comes to you, it's useful to reward her by scratching the base of her tail, which she can't reach herself.

On this day I was training Tara in a very congested area in Flushing, Queens, teaching her to come to me, and when she did so, I would scratch the base of her tail and repeat the words, "Come, Come, Come." The scratching along with the words helps the dog to associate the desired action with the scratch that she loved. I drew out the sound slowly and emphatically, "Come, Come, Come."

An old woman came toward us, and on hearing me, stopped in her tracks and glared at me, "Just what are you doing, young man?"

"I'm training my dog to come," I responded, unaware that she would think I meant a different meaning for the word.

"You're a no-good pervert. You shouldn't do that to a dog."

∞ *Be careful what you say and do in public places!*

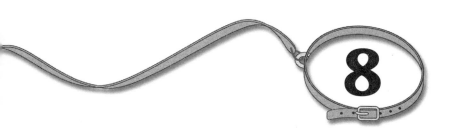

Howling at the Moon:
When All Else Fails, Pray Hard

DOGS AND WOLVES THRILL US when, sitting tall, they
look into the distance, open up their chests, and howl
at the moon. What does it all mean? Why does it evoke such
an awesome sense of splendor, majesty, and power? Is it a
call to the Great Spirit beyond dimensions of human percep-
tion to another sphere where Ultimate Reality abides, hearing
all, seeing all, and knowing all?

At one time or another, most of us experience extraordinary
moments in which, regardless of faith or lack thereof, we find
ourselves moved in the depths of our being to call out to God,
however we conceive God to be.

Like our canine brethren howling at the moon, we look
into the distance, open up our hearts, and call forth into the
void. When all else has seemed to fail, do we not find ourselves somehow—despite ourselves—striving to pray? Dogs
and wolves howl to call for a mate or for the pack in their
quest for companionship and food. From them, perhaps, we

might learn to reach beyond ourselves, to open our hearts and pray in whatever mode or manner fits us best.

The anecdotes that follow are not all about extreme moments, but they touch in some way upon extraordinary experiences that might impel us to pray or at least to look beyond appearances to a greater reality.

⌂ Geisty Saves the Day

by Theresa Mancuso

GEISTY WAS FINALLY PREGNANT and was drawing close to whelping time. Whenever she stirred in her crate beside my bed I awakened, thinking that perhaps the pups might be pressing on her bladder. When I opened my eyes at four that morning, only one eye could see. The vision in my left was cloaked with whiteness.

I didn't want to call anyone at such an hour. I put my head back down on the pillow and prayed as earnestly as I ever had in my entire life. "Dear God," I said, "please don't take away my sight."

Lifting my head again, I still could not see with my left eye. With my right I saw Geisty, longing to go outdoors. Panic rose within me but I continued to pray. Finally, my vision returned in that eye, crackling, like a TV screen starting up. I went to the doctor in the morning, and it seemed I needed surgery immediately. My vascular surgeon said that Geisty had saved the day.

"If you had not awakened for that dog to relieve herself," the doctor told me, "and if you had not moved your head, in all likelihood, the blood clot that blocked your vision temporarily might have remained there, making you permanently blind. Furthermore, it is quite possible that a complete stroke would have ensued some hours later with more disastrous effects. Your dog probably saved your life."

∞ *Just when you're most afraid and calling out for help, it might be that rescue has arrived and you just can't recognize it yet.*

⌂ Saying Goodbye to Jenna

by Audrey Elias

M Y FIRST DOG, JENNA, was twelve years old when one day we were walking around the block. Suddenly, she sat down. This began to happen frequently, and our vet said nerves in her spine were degenerating. In less than a month, Jenna went from being able to walk around the block to not being able to stand. So long as she could sit, we could slip a towel under her abdomen and hoist her to the curb to do her business. When I commanded her to sit, she wouldn't move at first so I would have to add a stern, "Bad dog!" Then she would struggle up, sad-eyed.

I realize I should have had Jenna put to sleep when she could no longer walk. But I couldn't bear to. She still seemed happy when I sat beside her and stroked her. When I began to suspect she was in pain, when her breathing had become quick and shallow, and she was no longer interested in food, I called our vet to come to euthanize her.

I made a great effort to remain calm since Jenna was affected by my moods. We moved her out to our deck because she loved the open air and the sight of passing squirrels. I spent a long time stroking her and talking to her quietly. When the vet came, I put Jenna's head into my lap, rubbed her ears, and praised her calmly and lovingly. I didn't allow myself to cry until the vet said, "She's gone."

∞ *When it's time to say goodbye, words and gestures fail us, but heart speaks to heart in ways we can't explain.*

⌂ Beyond Luck

by Mary Frenzel-Berra

I CALLED HER. She came charging out of the field, and the car hit her. It was a kid, hot-rodding down a private road where he didn't belong. She ran off yelping. The kid stopped. I should have been paying better attention, I thought, and he shouldn't have been there. Things flash through your mind, and one's first inclination is to blame.

I set out looking for her, calling, whistling, crying, crashing through brush, slogging in ditches and crawling through culverts, trying to *become* that dog so I could find her. I wanted to tell her I was sorry, even if she were dead. At dark, I quit looking to call the police, vets, animal shelters, and radio stations, describing her and offering rewards. Over and over, I relived the awful scene.

Then, about 10:30 P.M. there was a knock on the door. The kid was standing there.

"Your dog's outside," he said. "She came home. I heard you calling her. Tore me up." Then he turned and walked off.

The kid had probably followed me and hunkered down near my house, waiting for what neither of us quite knew would happen—the miracle of her finding her way home.

I think about that young man sometimes. Maybe he thinks about me, too. We were recipients of grace that day.

∞ *Miracles come to us unexpected, not because we deserve them, but because of the infinite hand of destiny.*

⌂ Dog Spelled Backwards Is God

by Dr. Nancy Bekaert

I TRULY BELIEVE that the dog is a higher being that is on this earth to teach mankind the meaning of unconditional love.

When my elderly friend's partner died, she was lost in grief and only wanted to join him. When she broke her hip and ended up in a nursing facility, she refused to eat and barely spoke. When I phoned her, she only mumbled in a voice barely audible, "I wish I could see Raffy before I die."

Riff-Raff (Raffy, to his friends) is my little black-and-white terrier. Einstein he is not, but he is an expert at unconditional love. I sent Mary Ann some photos of Raffy and promised that we would come. On our visit two weeks later, Mary Ann led the way from room to room introducing Raffy to all the patients and giving out some of the photos I'd sent to those she felt were particularly in need of his special brand of comfort.

Two weeks later, when I phoned, the nursing home staff said, "Mary Ann is no longer with us." I was happy to think that at least she had gotten her wish in seeing Raffy. I stopped by her house to offer condolences to her family. There, to my great surprise, I discovered Mary Ann herself, out in the back, gardening.

Raffy is now a certified therapy dog, and Mary Ann has adopted an older dog that she is training for his certification.

∞ *Unconditional love is God's blessing.*

⌂ Whom Can You Trust?

by Michael Marino

M Y FATHER-IN-LAW, BILL, was one of the first people to build on Bergen Beach in Brooklyn, in the early 1950s. There was a considerable amount of swampy land there that nobody thought was worth much at the time.

The area was home to a pack of feral dogs that kept to the shadows. They caused no problems to speak of and were hardly ever seen except when they hunted for food. My father-in-law was a generous and kind man. He took notice of the scrawny dogs that passed in tiny well-knit packs through the fields or scurried among the trees and shrubs close to the swamp, and he began to put food out for the feral dogs.

They came by day and kept their distance, eating whatever Bill provided. They came closer at night. Gradually, the dogs grew more confident. They seemed to know that they had discovered a friend. But still they grabbed whatever food he held out to them and quickly ran away, never lingering longer than it took to take whatever he offered. And then one day, a feral dog came back to offer Bill something in return.

For whatever reason may have prompted the feral dog to do so, it came right up to him and deposited a tiny puppy at his feet, which became Bill's first family dog in the new home.

∞ *Helping someone in need is blessed work, and you may well be rewarded.*

♠ Aurora and the Prairie Rattlesnake

by Catherine Raven Feher-Elston

I T WAS MID-JULY in the Cheyenne uplands, 6,000 feet up where the air is cooler, and we were off for our daily run in the sandstone hills—Aurora, the wolf; Denali, the Alaskan malamute; and I.

We drove into a breathtaking vista of mountains, forests, clouds, and grasslands. No breezes blew, but there was the blessed shade of pines. Aurora joyfully ran out, bounding far into the high dry grass. "Aurora, come," I called, and in a minute, she was beside me. I saw drops of blood on her right leg. Fear rose in my heart. I knew it must be a rattlesnake bite. We were an hour from the nearest vet. I sped down the dirt road and highway to the college at Lame Deer.

"My dog was bitten by a rattlesnake," I cried, rushing into the cafeteria for a bucket of ice. The men quickly helped. I ran to the van and packed her leg with ice. Unable to raise the local vet, I called two others and asked for treatment methods. A vet from twenty miles north returned my call. We hurried there, and he administered the first doses of steroids and amoxicillin. She needed to be dosed twice a day for the next four days and there was a chance of renal failure.

Aurora's leg swelled to three times normal size, but she never went into shock or lost her appetite. Beautiful Aurora recovered and is alive and well.

∞ *Accidents often bring us around to realizing what truly matters.*

⌂ An Awakening

by Neal C. Jennings

T EDDY WAS A beautiful golden retriever, a breed champion and holder of obedience titles. While his show and obedience career continued, he also became a therapy dog with Pets on Wheels of Scottsdale, Arizona. One of Teddy's greatest moments came when he and his human companion, DeEtte, were asked to visit a young boy who was in a coma.

This was the first time Teddy had visited anyone who showed such a lack of response. He was used to a lot of enthusiastic petting, hugging, and "thanks for coming" talk. He was in the usual spot, with his front paws on top of the metal rail at the side of the boy's bed. But all his tail wagging and paw padding on the side of the bed brought no reaction. The boy maintained his complete stillness, out of touch with the world.

Since Teddy was trained to bark on command, and the boy was reported to have had a golden-like dog some time in the past, his human said, "Speak." Teddy barked three times, always a no-no in the hospital. He was just a few feet from the boy's ear. To everyone's surprise the boy, who had not responded to stimuli since going in the coma, turned his head for a moment. His eyes fluttered, but did not open.

The boy's recovery came about gradually during the next few days.

∞ *A dog's voice, a child's smile, an elderly person's wink—how many hearts are lifted by momentary, passing little things.*

🏠 A Dog Star Is Born?

by Lori Sash-Gail

A S THE PROFESSIONAL dog trainer of Butchie, a virtually untrained bearded collie with scrumptious charm that recently got his first commercial for a flea-and-tick product, I needed to know all the tricks of the trade. Butchie's light green eyes and love for children got him the job. His yards of white and brown hair, giant pink tongue, and brown nose wooed the directors, but his airborne kissing nearly knocked them over. Butchie had charisma but no experience.

When I saw the giant movie trucks, lights, and caterers, reality hit and panic struck. I uttered the dog trainer's silent prayer, "Dear Lord, please make Butchie behave well today."

Butchie had to play checkers, read a story, have a birthday party, and kiss PJ, his nine-year-old female costar. Confidence is not my strong suit, and I wondered if Butchie could handle it.

"Kissing the child" seemed to be an easy task. I thought I had it in the bag—*wrong!* It was the most difficult one of the day. Butchie became bored and walked off the set. We solved the problem by smearing chicken baby food under PJ's chin. Voila! Twenty-five takes of dog licking child. Perfect!

I used a cream-cheesed index finger to focus Butchie on the camera for shots requiring him to look into the lens. At the end of the day, thoroughly caked with baby food, I went home feeling satisfied and successful.

🏠 Wolfsong in Brooklyn

by Theresa Mancuso

I DIDN'T KNOW I'd be a wolf lover until I reached midlife and became puppy parent to a black sable German shepherd, whom I named Grip. So many people told me that he looked wolfish that I was drawn slowly but surely into an ever-deepening fascination with Canis lupis. I began to read assiduously about wolves. I purchased an audiotape of wolves howling, a recording made in 1978 by F.H. Harrington. Harrington catalogued over twenty different wolf calls in a Minnesota wolf preserve. His observations indicated that each howl had its own significance to the pack.

The tape recording had great significance to my pack, too. When I played Harrington's tape in our cozy Brooklyn apartment one evening, Cara Mia, my two-year-old German shepherd bitch, was lying on the couch, listening intently. As the wolf pups began to yelp and whine, she raised her ears and became very alert. Then, almost with tenderness, Cara Mia started to croon softly. Her voice was gentle and soothing in response to those babies. A few moments later, the powerful howl of the alpha wolf filled the tiny darkened room. My ten-month-old shepherd pup, Grip, stood tall, arched his furry neck, and lifted high his beautiful sable head. He howled passionately, as if to match the call of the great gray wolf on tape. I felt the hair on the back of my neck rise up, and an incredible thrill filled my heart.

∞ *When wolves and dogs howl at the moon, perhaps they are calling from the depths of their being, to the Great Spirit and Maker of the Universe.*

⌂ Henry's Story

by Paul Sutton

T HERE HAD BEEN A SPATE of dog snatchings in our area recently, and a gorgeous six-month-old lurcher pup (that is, a crossbred hound dog) called Henry was taken from his garden near where I live. Henry was a delightful bouncy youngster full of life and energy. I enjoyed stroking him whenever I passed his gate. His owners were distraught and covered the area with posters offering £500 reward for any news about their kidnapped dog. It's just terrible not knowing what has happened to a lost animal. The heartsick owners also hired a pet detective to lead the search for poor, lost Henry.

Thankfully, they had had him microchipped because finally, a man driving past a rough area in London some twenty-five miles from Henry's home picked him up as a stray. Henry was in a dreadful state, scared, thin, and with a festering wound under his front leg. A vet scanned him and informed his now-ecstatic owners that he was safe. They had a wondrous reunion after six long and miserable weeks.

Henry is recovering well at home, a very lucky escape indeed. The police think he was taken for hare coursing and dumped because he was no good at it. By the look of him, you could see that he must have been badly treated by the dog thieves. Hopefully, however, Henry will make a full recovery and bounce back to the dog he was before. Some good things do happen!

∞ *Miracles remind us to work as if everything depends on us and to pray as if everything depends on God.*

🏠 The Bone Thief

by Theresa Mancuso

F OR ALL THREE of my dogs, the favorite goodie was a meaty bone straight from the Italian butcher. When I parked the van in front of United Meat Market, I could almost hear them draw in deep breaths, waiting for me to emerge with three huge trophies, marrowbones loaded with remnants of beef.

At home, each dog went immediately to its own crate to await bone delivery service. There's never been a fight about

---

food or bones in my pack. When the initial chew was over and there was no further reason to worry about bloody stains, the dogs were free to take their bones and enjoy them at leisure in their favorite spots. Inevitably, some time later, Cara Mia's wet nose and Geisty's inimitable chatter would interrupt me, complaining that their bones were missing. Quite mysteriously, too, since they were slow eaters and never could have finished off these enormous meaty bones in such a short time.

The mystery was solved when I went into the living room and found Grip on his pad, ecstatically gnawing at his bone with two more partially hidden beneath the elbow of his foreleg.

"Ah-ha!" I said. "What have we here?" A thumping tail and doggie grin was the only response. The girls stood back watching while I retrieved the stolen goods.

∞ *Accept your limitations, and choose your battles carefully.*

 ## ⌂ My Best Girl

by Louise Maguire

I HEARD ABOUT Bridget through friends, and she sounded like my sort of dog. Her human parents were divorcing and, at nine months, she needed a new home. We met on Valentine's Eve, and I immediately fell for her slim gingerbread and sable figure and her wayward charm. Her expressive ears were tipped forward, tulip style, then laid back politely like a rose.

I was told she needed training and exercise. What I didn't know was that she would develop long-term behavior and stress problems. When I fetched her home, she was subdued, confused, and sporting a perpetual serious frown on her pretty face. A week later, I finally heard her bark.

When she regained her usual energy, she showed classic symptoms of separation anxiety, shadowing me everywhere. Left alone even briefly, she scratched up carpets, scraped paintwork, chewed skirting boards, and urinated and defecated because of stress. Outside, during walks, Bridget yanked and lunged at her lead. If released, she would shoot off after distant dogs or complete strangers, especially children, ignoring my calls.

Although these problems are only memories today, they certainly didn't disappear overnight. And I had thought I was a good dog trainer! To celebrate Bridget's second birthday, I organized a private photo-shoot. There she is on film, now, posing like a dream, standing, sitting, lying down, in close-up, balanced on a log, alert but oh, so obedient. My best girl, that's Bridget.

∞ *Things have a way of turning out for the best if we put forth sufficient effort.*

⌂ The Miracle of Hope: Part 1

by Susan Rubin

I NAMED HER SPERANZA, Italian for "hope," and she
embodied the virtue after which she was named. It was
her third birthday, a beautiful March day. I decided to take
Speranza for a walk in the park before her party. Few cars
drove around there on weekends. Speranza was excellent off
leash, so I let her go, watching her majestic movements as she
roamed free. Her shiny, thick coat, tri-color markings, and
beautiful collie-shaped head looked regal in profile.

Speranza trotted happily beside me as we left the park an
hour later. Suddenly, a squirrel appeared and darted across a
perpendicular street. She was off chasing it fast. Out of nowhere,
a car came speeding up the street where Speranza was headed.
In frightening succession I heard screeching brakes, a loud thud,
and Speranza's pain-filled cry. My heart stopped. I screamed her
name and threw off my coat, running as fast as I could to her.

Speranza's torso was wrapped around the right front wheel
of the car. The driver, panicking, kept driving the car forward and
back, not seeming to understand that he was crushing my dog
under his wheels. I yelled for him to stop and called Speranza's
name. She managed to get up and drag herself to me at the side
of the road. Blood pouring from her mouth, she collapsed with
her head on my lap. In times like these we learn what we are
truly made of. I didn't name her "Hope" for nothing.

∞ *In the face of traumatic events, the real meaning of love and
hope come to the fore.*

⌂ The Miracle of Hope: Part 2

by Susan Rubin

I N THE ANIMAL HOSPITAL, Speranza received a blood transfusion and X rays. They said she had a concussion and perhaps brain damage. She was bleeding internally, and they didn't have the means to determine the cause or to stop it. Her back and ribs had sustained fractures, and she was unable to use one leg. The doctor told me she might not live, and, if she did, that she might not walk again. I listened carefully, but clung to hope.

The biggest danger she faced was the possibility of a heart attack that would kill her instantly due to deep bruising in her chest. I stroked her through her cage. She seemed so fragile, but I knew how strong she was—I had seen her act bravely many times to protect those she loved.

I leaned toward her, telling her I knew she had a strong heart that would beat the odds. Speranza seemed to understand. I visited every day. When doctors said she was slipping away, when they said that even if she could walk again, she might forever need to wear a diaper, my hope did not waiver. Neither did my girl's.

Today, more than three years later, Speranza has made a full recovery. She safely bounds, like an antelope, through the hills near our home. As I type this, she is looking at me, full of hope that I will share my nearby snack. Life won out against the experts' predictions of doom. Speranza creates more love in my world every day.

∞ *Never give up hope, no matter what.*

⌂ Lobo, Scout Dog

by Anthony Jerone

L OBO WAS FROM CALIFORNIA, about a year old when he joined me in service in the army. A scout dog and its point man go ahead of the troops. As a scout dog, Lobo detected mines, booby traps, and ambushes by air-scenting. Air-scenting dogs detect metal, wire, or body odor up ahead. Dogs recognize 250,000 different odors; they sense variations in human scent caused by secretions based on diet and other factors. They have amazingly sensitive hearing. They can hear the wind blowing against a wire that you can't see with the naked eye.

Lobo and I were in the Mekong Delta, twelve miles from North Vietnam. Lobo air-scented and gave the alert, bobbing his nose up and down, meaning that an ambush was waiting up ahead about 500 to 700 meters. I'd give the alert to air support, using the clock system. With Lobo worked into the wind, I radioed in that the ambush was at 12:00 if his nose pointed straight ahead. If his nose pointed to the right, the enemy was at 3:00, whereas nose left meant 9:00. Once we told them our location and the whereabouts of the ambush, the air force would bomb it to bits.

In the Mekong Delta, we worked with Flower Power, the Ninth Infantry Division. All around us there were rice paddies and danger. Six months later we went north to Quantri. We served with the Fifth Mechanized Division, called Red Diamond. Lobo was a great scout; he saved lots of lives.

∞ *Dedication and loyalty make for guardian angels.*

⌂ Becoming a Doggie Midwife

by Theresa Mancuso

I T WAS MY FIRST TIME whelping puppies. Brother Peter, who had given me careful instructions, would be there to guide me. Not only was I a new dog foster mom, Natasha, my German shepherd, was having her first litter.

I could understand that night why fathers pace so nervously! After what seemed an interminable length of labor, the first birth was starting to happen, but alas, number one pup had a huge head and Natasha seemed unable to deliver. Diligently and gently, I eased the passage by maneuvering my fingers gently around Natasha's opening, careful not to hurt her or to damage the puppy's crowning head. It came forth at last, but poor Natasha was still a bit confused and did not try to break the sack or lick her baby. The pup was not breathing. We wrapped it in a clean towel and rubbed it gently but vigorously, making careful movements up and down to evacuate the blocked passageway. Mucous rose and vacated the puppy's lungs and throat. The little whelp whimpered in a tiny voice. We settled the puppy against Natasha's body and waited for the delivery of its littermates.

After that, Natasha knew exactly what to do. The rest of her babies came at twenty-minute intervals, easily and rapidly, with no problems. She was a splendid mom. Being midwife for my dog was for me one of the most spiritual experiences of a lifetime, precious, priceless, and magnificent, a time of total interconnectedness with the natural universe.

∞ Spiritual birth, our journey to enlightenment, happens again and again. In the darkness of spiritual night, we must labor diligently for our own re-birth.

....

⌂ Wilson Rising

by Scott Cohen

A
FTER HIS SURGERY, Wilson needed daily care. My boss, a big-hearted curmudgeon, said, "Sure, I like dogs, it's people I'm not too sure about," and let me bring him to work. For six weeks I smuggled him past the security guard and into my office, where he slept on a towel under my desk. Twice a day I would quietly close my door, place him on my lap, and perform the twenty minutes of exercises that a holistic dog therapist had prescribed.

In addition to exercises, I gave Wilson hydrotherapy, his "swimming lessons." Wilson wasn't too keen on his routine: exercises four times a day, supplements, swimming, massage, acupuncture, more exercise. My friends joked that I'd be taking him for ballet and violin lessons next.

Because he couldn't walk, my dog taught me a new language. Lip-licking meant he wanted water, sniffing the air signaled hunger, and a short growl indicated he needed to relieve himself. Six weeks after the surgery, Wilson still couldn't raise himself, and I was growing discouraged.

One day I went to deliver something down the hall, leaving my office door ajar. As I was talking, someone yelled, "Hey, there's a dog in here!" Turning around, I saw that Wilson had followed me down the hall on three awkward legs.

Now he walks normally, though he's shaped like an "S" and sometimes gets his hind legs tangled up in front of his forepaws when he runs. He still won't be doing ballet anytime soon.

∞ *The courage to endure despite the odds is the stuff of heroism. Our survival on this planet may one day well demand the same of us, nothing less.*

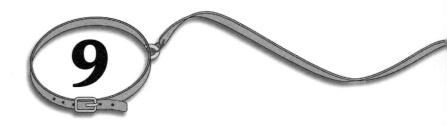

Bury Those Bones:
Making Decisions and Sticking to Them

INTELLIGENCE AND FREE WILL are fundamental character-istics of human nature. In conjunction with the powerful force generated by emotional inclination (otherwise known as desire), the mind and will constantly formulate and move us to carry out important decisions every day of our lives. Some decisions and choices are relatively easy. But making some decisions and sticking to them can be very difficult.

Some of the anecdotes that follow might tear at your heart-strings. Dog people know this kind of pain, and they know it well. But notwithstanding the heartaches of dog-related deci-sions, our canine friends are often a solid comfort and source of solace in the face of other decisions required of us by life. Dog lovers choose to have dogs regardless of the cost, a deci-sion that often underpins decisions of a far different nature.

Observation indicates that dogs, too, make real decisions. Perhaps they do not anguish over them as humans do, but doggie decisions are no less valuable in the nature of canine being and behavior. They sometimes make us wonder whether humans have very much underestimated the real possibilities of the canine mind. The dog that decides to save its owner at the cost of its own life is probably acting from instinct, but is there perhaps another operative deep down underneath? Could your dog *refuse* to be your friend? Could your dog choose to protect its *own* life rather than save yours? Who's to say?

As a dog owner and lover of all things canine, I will always be grateful for the decisions I have made in favor of my canine family, keeping them regardless of the consequences, for indeed, their love and fidelity have been a stalwart fortress against the vicissitudes of life. If I had to choose it all again, I'd let myself go to the dogs every time.

⌂ A Clear Potential Danger

by Irene Smith

S HE WAS DANCING down the middle of a busy avenue, dragging her leash, having a wonderful time. I drafted two passers-by to stop traffic and knelt on the asphalt, opening my arms to her. She came right into them. Lucy was a seven-month-old pit bull terrier with the classic wedge-shaped head, white with black markings and a black bull's eye around one eye. She was winsome and beautiful but completely untrained except in one disturbing respect. She was inappropriately aggressive toward children. I learned from a ubiquitous sidewalk dweller in my East Harlem neighborhood that Lucy had been trained to menace children by the drug dealer who bred her. His collection method was to threaten to sic the dog on the children of his debtors who failed to pay their drug bills. Lucy had been put out on the street because she wasn't aggressive enough.

With her incredibly strong locking jaw, Lucy represented a clear potential danger to children. Consultations with several groups dedicated to rehabilitating such animals were discouraging. In their opinion, Lucy would always be a catastrophe on its way to happening. Pit bull terriers are a challenge to train, but once they learn something, they never forget it.

The choice was clear. With a grieving heart, I made arrangements for Lucy to be humanely put down. We cried before, during, and after, mourning another innocent victim. I believe I did the right thing. The odds that Lucy would maul a child at some time in her life were just too high.

∞ *Sometimes hope is not enough, and we must make a difficult choice.*

···········

⌂ Thy Kingdom Come

by Theresa Mancuso

W HEN MY ANIMAL rescuer friend, Irene, and I renewed our friendship after some years, she told me that she had just taken in a beautiful German shepherd dog whose name was King and who needed a permanent home. Poor King had spent too much time tied up in a yard all alone or left to fend for himself in a concrete alley, untrained at ten months of age.

When I came to see him, King spread out on Irene's bed and several tiny kittens crawled over him and around him, nestling on his large front paws. I fell in love.

Then I remembered the numerous problems I had already encountered during the past thirteen years keeping dogs in my apartment. Our struggles for survival were wearing me down. And the co-op board had established a two-animal limit on all apartments—a quota I had reached. Sadly, I left King behind. Irene assured me that things usually work out and I ought not worry. I worried anyway, night and day.

Another week passed and then King found his kingdom— or rather, he let kingdom come, and it did. A loving family welcomed King into their home. He revels there delightfully at play with Seilius, a terrier, enjoying their large backyard. The dogs have two teenaged brothers of the human variety to love. What could be better for King than a home and family of his own?

∞ *Sometimes, hard choices are necessary. Things may work out anyway.*
....

🏠 Aggressive Dog

by Jolanta Benal

MY IZZY is a Basic Yellow Dog. She's polite, but never forward. When someone to whom she hasn't been properly introduced begins to stroke and scratch, she quietly withdraws.

Izzy has lived with us for more than five years, going to Prospect Park almost every day, and unlike those argumentative types whose owners claim that theirs is an alpha dog, she's hardly ever had a fight. She has a nice line in reprimands, though. One morning, while she was investigating a patch of grass that needed marking, a big male Lab slipped up behind her and started to hump her.

Izzy slid out from underneath.

He humped again.

Izzy slid out and shot him a look.

He humped again.

Izzy slid out and curled her lip.

He humped again.

Izzy slid out and snapped at him.

I have to admit that I was rooted to the spot. I thought, "Well, he's not gonna do that again." But he did—just one last time. Izzy slid out with a snarl-roar I'd never heard before and brought him to the ground. No is no!

The Lab's owner looked up, at last, from his latte, and said, "Jeez! What an aggressive dog!"

∞ *There are times when you simply must assert yourself!*

....

🏠 Promises to Keep

by Theresa Mancuso

I VOWED THAT IF EVER I COULD, I would surely get her back. I had been compelled by monastic obedience to forfeit Natasha. Her first two litters had not been exactly what the breeding program required, and when she developed uterine problems that prohibited reproduction, her life as a brood bitch came to an abrupt end. A park security guard named George took her to be his helper.

Some years later, George stopped in with her. I opened the front door and called out: "Tash!" Released, she bolted over the bushes and leaped into my arms, her front paws locked around my neck in an embrace of steel.

George said that for a week after he had taken her, Natasha was unwilling to eat or move. He took her into his own bed and fed her by hand. Eventually, George told me, Natasha grew to love him and to enjoy patrolling the park. But when it was time for them to go, she refused to leave me. Crying, I walked her to the car and watched them drive away. I saw her one more time. Saying goodbye was so painful that this time I decided I would never attempt to visit her again. Someday, I promised myself, I would buy her. When I left the monastery in 1981, I called George.

"I am so very sorry, Sister," George said. "Natasha died last winter. The park committee just erected a bronze monument in her honor that says: 'To Natasha, the Lady of the Park'."

∞ *Decisions of the heart cannot be questioned, but sometimes fate intervenes and neither can they be carried out. Trust yourself, and accept the destiny that lies before you.*

⌂ The Rio Rescue

by Irene Smith

RIO WAS A WELL-BEHAVED DOG, responsive to commands and well mannered on the leash. One morning, however, as we turned the corner into a large yard behind the local high school, Rio turned into a bad dog, pulling at the leash, literally dragging me along. Finally he broke away, jumped a four-foot iron fence, and disappeared into the early morning mist. I ran behind him, disturbed by this behavior and half angry, half fearful that he would run away and get lost.

I couldn't jump the fence, so I had to go around to the gate. I saw him circling what looked like a bag of garbage. Assuming that he had intuited some forbidden and disgusting snack, I shouted, "Rio, no!" He ignored me.

I finally reached him and, to my horror, realized that Rio had found the body of a young woman, wrapped in black garbage bags, lying still on the grass. I could see she was badly injured, one leg turned back at an unnatural angle, her face bloody and bruised. Her breathing was shallow, almost imperceptible. I ran for a phone, knowing that Rio would stay beside her until help arrived.

The young woman had been brutally raped and beaten, invisible to passersby on this foggy morning, desperately in need of help. Had she been left there unattended for another hour, she surely would have died of exposure and her injuries. Instead, she fully recovered, and she and Rio have become part of our East Harlem folklore.

∞ *Don't second-guess your gut-level instinct.*

⌂ Maya's Mission

by Heather Cosgrave

MAYA DIED Wednesday night at her home, cradled in the arms of her new mom. No sound marked her tragic passing, but traces of her memory are left behind, little outfits and dog treats, a fancy dog bed with the outline of her body on it. How could she have gone so soon?

We took her body to be cremated and picked out the special urn where her ashes would rest, a fitting tribute. Three months. That's how long her rescuer had her. Three months. That's how long we had her. Ten days. That's how long she was the center of her new mom's universe in her own forever home.

Maya had survived an abusive home that left her scarred physically, mentally, and emotionally. Maya bore wounds no pup should ever have to endure. In human terms, she should have had so much more time to enjoy the happiness of her new home with all its promise. But perhaps her evolved spirit had indeed sufficient time to accomplish its mission on Earth. Finally, if just for a little while, Maya found the gift that only love can give. Her mission, then, was well fulfilled. The healing touch that soothes the troubled spirit, the warm bed and good food, the loving face to kiss, and the someone kind who deeply cares—this is what Maya finally found in her journey. Maya's life may have been just long enough to find her own forever home and leave her mark on everyone who loved her.

∞ *Think deeply on the real meaning of your existence. Why*

are you here at all? Live each moment in the light of your
authentic mission.
....

⌂ Tabou to the Rescue

by Louise Maguire

TABOU THE VETERAN BOXER lay at the feet of my visitors snoring at intervals. Outside splendid untouched
mounds of glorious fresh snow sloped temptingly.

"Let's go sledding!" somebody said, and the idea was irresistible. I found three battered trays, and we raced outside. I
shut the door on Tabou's indignant face, knowing his vendetta
against metal objects like wheelbarrows. So he moved from dining room windows, to sitting room windows, to the French windows, smearing each at muzzle level with a line of his heavy
sighs. His wrinkled, doleful face insisted this was no way to
treat a canine gentleman. My friend Shona, who was basically
reared by three German shepherds, was the easy mark.

"We're being really mean," Shona said. "I'm going to let him
out. We can out-sled him anyway."

She unwisely opened the nearest French window, and like
some terrible cartoon character, Tabou galumphed out and immediately switched into guard-dog mode. These slippery spinning
objects had no place in his garden, and he would prove it.

He was determined to capture the trays, especially when
we were aboard. Three minutes later, both Shona and Alex had

---

abandoned their vehicles, retreated inside, and hastily shut the French windows. For a change, I saw worried human faces pressed against the glass as I failed to wrestle my tray out of Tabou's teeth.

Back inside, Tabou reverted to his peaceful self.

"Look," said Alex. "He's sound asleep already!"

"After foiling three dangerous kidnappers, he can afford to relax," I explained.

∞ *Don't be swayed from what you know is right by others who might not have as much understanding of the situation as you do.*

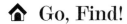 Go, Find!

by Theresa Mancuso

OUR DOGS WILL NEVER be search-and-rescue heroes, but they've got determination when it comes to practicing. No matter where my friend Maxine and I take my Abby and her Beatrice and Willie, "Go, Find" is their favorite escapade. One day Max decided to climb a fir tree and took her position high up.

The dogs were hot on the trail, weaving in and out, eager for the prize. Max watched the spectacle from her airborne seat without giving away her hiding place. I, on the other hand, newly convalesced from a broken foot, found it difficult to traipse along behind the search team. Circling the woods, they ran forward and backward, sideward and headlong into tall grass where I lost sight of them until they emerged on the other side, galloping.

"Go, find!" I called excitedly as they circled back far from the brink of defeat. "Get those noses going!" I commanded.

Up went the twittering noses of the large German shepherd, the feisty stubby basset, and the wiry white terrier mix. They scanned the air, trying to pick up the current of a wafting scent that might direct their course. Then, like a bullet, someone caught it on the wind, and off they went, one behind the other.

I heard Max call out enthusiastic praise to Willie, the terrier mix, whose paw was heading upward on a tree trunk, just below where Maxine perched, some fifteen feet skyward. She had beaten the best of them. Willie had her prize!

∞ *Never quit when you're on the chase. Stick it out when the going gets rough.*
....

🏠 Iditarod Dog

by Lynzie Bacchus

MY FATHER AND I went to Togo, Minnesota, for dogsled training with Jamie Nelson. I was *absolutely not* to bring a dog home. As I got better acquainted with Jamie, I started helping with the puppies. Standing outside the door of the puppy pen, I watched a muddy black-and-white female Alaskan husky with ears too big for her head. It was love at first sight. I named her Wilo.

The more time went on, the more I knew I had to bring Wilo home. Wilo seemed to know I liked her best and always pushed the other pups aside to reach me. I finally convinced my dad to let me have her. I brought Wilo home, and we've been best buddies ever since.

When Wilo was a year old, I started running her in lead position, and she was a natural. During training for the Junior Iditarod of 2003, I put Wilo in lead at the start of the race. She was awesome. She let me know when a team was approaching from two miles back. On the last stretch, the team was giving out and wanted to quit, but every time they'd lie down, I called out, "All right, Wilo, girl, let's go."

Wilo would pull the whole nine-dog team up and keep them going. At the very end, it seemed like Wilo couldn't go on, but she forced herself to keep the team going. Without her, I wouldn't have finished the race.

∞ *A true leader never gives up.*

⌂ To Grip or Not to Grip. That Is the Question.

by Theresa Mancuso

D OMINIC DONAVON SHOWED ME a pup he called Grip, a stocky, confident black sable German shepherd male. He was clearly a magnificent dog. I asked Dom to put the puppy into a crate in Elli's car while we negotiated the deal and signed the paperwork.

As I commenced to sign the purchase contract, I felt an uneasy lump in my throat, and suddenly I couldn't breathe. "I can't do this," I said. "I can't buy this puppy."

"No problem," Dominic said with a smile. His partner, Rick, suggested that we view a video of Grip's father, Natan vom Blauen Engel, son of Held Ritterberg, a famous East German dog. We viewed the video, and I began to reconsider.

"You know what, Dom? Let me see that contract again." I signed it. Then, as I was writing my check, I felt my breath imperiled once more. My chest tightened.

"I can't do this, Dom." Dominic brought Grip back into the house. The puppy circled the table and came straight to me. He laid his big blocky head in my lap. My heart skipped a beat. I wrote the check and took the dog home with me.

For twelve and a half years, Grip von der Starken was the best friend I ever had. I never met in my entire life a being quite like Grip, my special canine son. I always felt that one day Grip would unzip his dog suit and say, "Hey, Mom, I was a *real boy* all the time."

∞ *When you can't make up your mind, listen to your heart.*
When you can't hear your heart, listen deeper to your soul.
You'll know what's best for you.

⌂ Returned to Sender

by Lori Sash-Gail

I CAN'T RESIST; I send dogs to people I love. Misty was a
four-pound, black-and-tan Pomeranian that I hand-delivered
to my seventy-seven-year-old Grandma Mary.

Misty was cantaloupe shaped, with black fuzzy hair so
thick it spread horizontally from her body. Her eyes were like
coffee beans, framed by arched eyebrows. She had a black juju
nose and a watermelon tongue that curled upwards like gum.
Her tiny mouse ears perked up when you said, "Time to eat!"
Except for her tail, which she carried over her back like a
skunk, it was hard to tell back from front.

For six years, Grandma and I spoke weekly about her joy
in Misty. Grandma spoke of Misty's love of laps, not just the
kind you sit in but the kind you run—round and round, in the
garage. Grandma would run after Misty, trying to get her into
the house. Neighbors asked Grandma about the "black squirrel"
she was chasing. Grandma taught Misty to sit and stay. "Get a
life; get a dog." That was Grandma's motto.

I thought my spunky Grandma would live forever, but she
died in January, and as I promised I would, I brought Misty

home to Nyack. Misty spins in excited circles as she watches me prepare her food. Her appetite is unparalleled. After years of eating Grandma Mary's stuffed cabbage, she has become one herself. It's an honor to take care of Grandma's sole companion, "returned to sender," a full-circle gift.

∞ *Keeping promises isn't always easy, but it's an important part of sticking to decisions we made in the past.*

⌂ Morph, a Long-Suffering and Courageous Dog

by Wendy Halling

MORPH WAS THE bravest and most loyal German shepherd you'd ever hope to meet. He battled ill health all his life until he died in 2002 following his tenth gastric torsion. Allergic to grass, dog food, dandelions, and other common things, he couldn't be desensitized, so he lived on steroids, without which the itch would drive him nearly mad. Weekly baths were the routine, with umpteen pills and potions to keep him alive.

After his third gastric torsion in three months, the vet removed his spleen. A year of relatively good health followed, and his walks in the country and on the beach resumed, but we dreaded the next gastric torsion, knowing it would be a race to the vet's office to save him. Time and again, our vets brought Morph back from the brink.

His final battle happened just after a lovely holiday in Wales. Morph loved the rock pools and although he got tired, he never showed it. Not long after we returned, Morph went into a continuous torsion. We made the heartbreaking decision to put him to sleep. He went in my arms, licking my tears as he slipped peacefully away.

Morph's veterinary bills totaled nearly £12,000, but luckily, he was insured. We think of him often. Our new puppies have some of his characteristics, but they can never replace our dear friend.

∞ *It is not ours to decide when we've had enough; but for our dogs and other pets, the greatest love often requires a terrible mercy, putting them to sleep.*

⌂ Denial?

by Lori Sash-Gail

DENIAL IS MY FRIEND. When I was thirty-five years old, my father gave me the shock of my life: "You were always too tall to be a dancer." I had danced for ten years, never suspecting!

When Edna asked me to train her toy poodle, Chablis, to become a pet therapy dog, I had my doubts. Chablis clung to

Edna's lap, shook when keys dropped, and shied away from people. How would she become accustomed to wheelchairs, walkers, banging, bumping, and rough petting? But I could never formulate the words "not suitable." Instead, I sunk my head deeply into the sand. Seven months later, Chablis became a certified therapy dog.

I'm now training her sister. Chardonnay assumes the frozen-rabbit response to terrors such as laughter. I decided that she could take Chablis' place in an ad. All Chardonnay had to do was let the model hold her. She behaved like a cross between a wild bird and an unhappy cat getting a bath, arms and legs extended straight out, screeching. Eventually, they got the shot, and by then I was the one who needed a shot. The assistant christened me the "poodle whisperer." I never wanted to hear the word "poodle" whispered again.

With denial stronger than ever and now eight years out of shape, I still attend dance class. A question greets me: Could I do a doggie modern dance with my new, untrained dog for their concert?

"Sure," I frothed at the mouth, "I'd love to!" (They said I was too tall for their other dances. Who told them?)

∞ *Never let reality interfere with accomplishing the things you really want to do!*

Barks, Yelps, and Growls:
Develop a Positive Attitude

FOR MORE THAN TWELVE YEARS, I shared my life and a Brooklyn apartment with three German shepherds. I maintained a fairly upbeat and happy attitude about life, even though their daily need for exercise required me to give up many a morning's alternate activity to take them to the beach or the woods. I loved the opportunity to forget I was a city slicker, and I learned to sing and laugh amidst the barks, yelps, and growls, far from the noise of Brooklyn's crowded streets.

On whatever path you find yourself in your journey through life, you need to recognize opportunities for happiness and pursue them. Happiness is the thing you carry deep within, available to you in every circumstance, even the most difficult, if you can only muster up a positive attitude.

On our approach to the open spaces of Floyd Bennett Field or the beaches at Far Rockaway, just as soon as my car full of dogs would catch the first sniff of airborne smells arising from the ocean or fields, they would come alive in a medley of noisy yelps and barks, sometimes interspersed with a growl or two as they nudged and pushed each other aside to get the best view. The scent of sand, beach, and woodland must have tantalized them because their voices grew more and more shrill with excitement. Exhausted from their jaunt, they returned home with delighted smiles on their doggie faces, eyes drooping with fatigue. If anything can make a dog feel positive about life, it's fun and frolic in an open field or a cool, refreshing jaunt along the beach or a swim in the ocean.

Find what you need to sustain a positive attitude. It will support you in every endeavor and sustain you in every crisis. It will enrich your mind and strengthen your spirit. A positive attitude is the surest security in a world where nothing is secure. The only thing that is untouchable by all the events of life is how we, ourselves, choose to look upon them.

⌂ Chickenhearted

by Jolanta Benal

THE FEATHERLESS BIPEDS in my house don't eat a whole lot of meat. But sometimes a chicken comes with neck and giblets intact, and if you're not cooking them for yourself, what are you going to do? Certainly you can't throw them out—not when the dogs are sitting politely in the kitchen doorway, wagging their tails, with one of them reminding you that she used to live on the street, where she was very, very hungry?

This makes great practice for teaching dogs to wait until they are released. Put the dog into a sit. Hold the dog bowl over the dog's head, and place the chicken heart into the bowl. Lower the bowl, and raise it again if the dog breaks the sit. Dogs that hold the sit correctly get to enjoy chicken hearts, and owners of such dogs find themselves on the slippery slope to a raw diet.

Hence, my expertise in the festive variety meats: chicken gizzards, duck wings, pig snouts, tripe, chicken backs and necks (priced reasonably, you think, at nine cents a pound, until you see all the fat that's been stuffed into the bottom of the package where you can't see it till you get home). There's rabbit, organic lamb kidneys, lamb tongue, and huge beef heart. For two dollars, the butcher in my neighborhood will sell me a cow femur, cut into as many pieces as I want. At a buck per knucklebone, that makes the cheapest party I have ever held, which is just as well since the guests' manners leave much to be desired.

∽ *Think (and eat) outside the box. Experience new cuisines and different cultures with an open mind.*

🏠 The Pastor's Barn

by Mary Rodgers

O NE SATURDAY AFTERNOON, I took my dog, Killer, on my
visit with the pastor and his wife. When we drove up to the
parsonage, the two of them were waiting outside to greet us. As
soon as Killer jumped out of the car, he made a beeline for the
barn and the horses out back. The pastor and his wife knew very
well what was going to happen, but I didn't.

One of the parishioners had a youngster whose horse
had recently died. When the boy asked the pastor if the horse
would go to heaven, the pastor had reassured him with a kindly
response, "Why, yes, of course he will."

The child said, "Wherever the horses go, that's where I
wanna go when I die. If heaven doesn't have room for horses,
it doesn't have room for me." Well, that's just how I feel, too.
Wherever my dogs and cats are, that's where I want to be. On
this particular day, however, my dog, Killer, may not yet have
reached heaven in the pastor's barn—but he probably thought
he had. When I was finally ready to go, I called him. I knew
he was coming long before I saw him because of the smell.

We drove home with the car windows down. I carried
Killer into the house straight to the bathtub and while I bathed
him several times, he stood in the tub, fast asleep, thoroughly
pleased with his adventure in the manure pile.

∞ *Between now and heaven, we've all got plenty of manure
piles to face. A positive attitude might change the stench to per-
fume or, at least, make it livable.*

⌂ Turning Failure into Success

by Theresa Mancuso

TWO MEN IN THE Schutzhund club offered me $5,000 for my black sable German shepherd, Grip; they considered him prime material. In training, Grip performed the exercises, carrying them out with fine precision. But I wouldn't part with my beloved Grippinski for any amount of money. I would work him and show him myself.

We went to face a judge to pursue an elementary Schutzhund title, the "B." During the heeling exercise, we veered off toward the left, which made me tense. As we proceeded (slightly askew), Grip sensed my tension. He leaped on my back, all ninety-six pounds of him, and locked his front paws around my neck and shoulders. Then he pulled his rear feet and legs completely up and off the ground, so I found myself wearing him like a cloak. The audience laughed wildly.

In another exercise, each dog must remain on a long down/stay while the handler advances forty paces forward and keeps his back to the dog as the next dog goes through the paces of heeling. As I walked forty paces forward, I saw snickering in the audience. Finally, the judge said, "Theresa, retrieve your dog." I turned to get Grip, but he was already there. He had belly-crawled forty paces to reach me, still on his tummy.

We were dismissed from the Schutzhund ring without our "B." But I wrote a story that was published in *Dog World* magazine entitled, "How We Failed Our 'B.'" It earned us $500.

∞ *You may be able to turn failure into success when you keep your eye on the prize. And if the prize changes, pursue it anyway.*
....

⌂ Whisper's Operation

by Paul Sutton

EARLY IN 2003, I had a very worrisome time with Whisper. The vet found two lumps on her side and decided to remove them for analysis. The day of Whisper's operation was one of the longest of my life. When I rang, they told me she was coming around and I could collect her later. When I asked about the lumps, I was told that someone would speak to me when I picked her up. Whisper had a large bald patch on her side and two impressive-looking wounds. When she heard me speaking in the waiting room, she started to howl. I recognized the sound of her voice immediately and nearly started crying again.

Oh, the relief I felt when I was told the lumps were benign! I felt as if a great weight had been removed from my shoulders. I don't apologize for being overly emotional about it; animal lovers understand what it's like.

It's amazing how dogs recover after surgery. Whisper lay on the front seat of the car with her head in my lap (bliss) all the way home. The sun was shining on her adorable face. When we arrived back at home, Whisper had a look round to see if there was anything to eat, had a mooch in the garden, and totally ignored the lovely fresh towel bed I had made for her on the settee! Spoiled, my dog? Who said that?

∞ *Bounce back from life's crises and be grateful for what you have.*
....

♠ Ugly and the Waterbed

by Gail Smart

UGLY, MY SMART WHITE BOXER, was lying totally still. At just three years of age, his annual check-up showed up a severe heart defect. Now he was recovering from a risky anesthetic following investigative procedures undertaken to find the cause of his problems and, perhaps, a way to stabilize him. The hospital was especially busy at the time, so I was left to monitor his recovery.

Ugly had not moved since I went in with him. He lay there on the waterbed, immobile, but his breathing appeared regular. I had instructions to call for the cardiologist as soon as the dog started to come around. When the specialist looked in and asked how he was doing, Ugly still hadn't moved, but otherwise he was okay. Upon hearing my voice, Ugly's tail wagged heartily and he opened one blurry eye. When he saw me there beside him, he shut it tight again and continued sleeping. Nothing like a waterbed for a comfortable snooze!

According to Ugly's prognosis, he had a fifty-fifty chance of surviving the night. His condition worsened when he was given the first drug that was supposed to help him. Happily, however, the next drug was successful. Ugly has gone on for more years than ever thought possible with his catalogue of disasters.

∞ *Think positive and you often get positive back. Think negative, and the same befalls you.*

⌂ Dixie Does Therapy

by Ali Moore

DIXIE'S FORMER OWNERS gave her up because she didn't get along with other dogs—more specifically, it was a particular boxer that gave her trouble. In her defense (and I'm not fond of fighters, either) Dixie relates much better to humans than to dogs. I honestly think that Dixie believes she *is* human. She seems to have a keen sense of fashion. Her own English bulldog coat makes a bold statement—faux tiger!

After staying with us for a while, Dixie found her perfect parents. William and Susan were looking for a dog-child to spoil and shower with love. They didn't have any other dogs, so it looked like this could be a match made in heaven.

This happy family has joined us for all of our Bulldawg Rescue reunions. Though not wild about hanging out with the other canines, Dixie is always eager to be fussed over by the humans. She also loves being a contestant in the annual canine costume contest. This fashion guru must plan months in advance. Year after year she wows us with her up-to-the-minute, runway attire. I'd love to see her closet!

I recently learned from Susan that Dixie passed the battery of tests to become a certified therapy dog, and they have begun visiting nursing homes and assisted living facilities. Thanks to her new parents' positive attitude, Dixie has been able to foster her love of fashion and find her niche in life. This style star is a lover—not a fighter.

∞ *A little bit of understanding goes a long way.*

🏠 A Debutante Named Daisy

by Ali Moore

FROM THE MINUTE I met Miss Daisy, I knew she needed to own a little girl. She was a true lady who wanted nothing more than to attend tea parties and play dress-up. But that would have to wait.

Daisy came into rescue with heartworm, a disease that is preventable but can also be deadly if not treated. She also suffered from a torn cruciate ligament, a knee injury common in English bulldogs. Both problems would require a six- to eight-week recovery period. Our vet felt that it would be easiest for Daisy to have both her ailments treated simultaneously so she could recover from both at the same time.

While we awaited the new orthopedic tool that our vet had ordered for Daisy's surgery, the perfect little girl for Daisy came along. Rachael and her mom had a spotless application and raving vet references. They passed our home inspection with flying colors, and when they came to visit Daisy, it was love at first sight. This match was meant to be.

We let them take Daisy home to await her heartworm treatment and surgery. We felt that the love and stability that they would provide would give Miss Daisy the incentive to recover more quickly.

It worked! After eight weeks of TLC, spoiling, and physical therapy provided by Rachael and her mom, our vet gave Daisy a clean bill of health. Daisy is now thriving, swimming and running without pain, enjoying being the debutante that she is.

∞ *Love is the best medicine, the strongest motivation, and the quickest cure.*
....

 ⌂ Abby Gets Fired

by Theresa Mancuso

I WAS WEARING A hand-me-down community service jacket with our agency's emblem on it. Probation officers wore jackets and T-shirts like what I had on when they went into the field to supervise community-service work crews. A youthful

---

sixty-three-year-old, I could pass for a P.O., and Abby loved pretending she was an official K9 service dog.

I had my supervisor's permission to bring Abby to work with me in order to accommodate the painters in my apartment. The security guards acknowledged our arrival with a nod of the head. Abby rode the elevator like a pro. Up we went; Abby and I couldn't have been happier. I settled Abby down with a large dog bone and sat at my computer. Several colleagues passed my office on their way to the mailroom next door. They smiled and spoke to Abby, who wagged her tail effusively in cordial greeting, the picture of professional decorum.

Before the morning ended, however, the deputy commissioner had informed me himself that Abby must leave. I felt miserably betrayed by my colleagues. Someone must have complained about Abby's peaceful presence, and although I didn't know who it was, obviously the call had gone straight to the top, right to the Commissioner's office.

Our long walk to the subway station was sad for me, but for Abby it was a joyful continuation of her delightful morning out of the house and off to work with Mommy. Abby might have gotten fired, but as far as she was concerned, it was a glorious day at the office.

∞ *It's all a matter of perspective. Try to see things positively, no matter how flustered and upset you may be.*

⌂ Shandy Has His Day

by Louise Maguire

L IZ AND HENRY were first-time dog owners inspired by television ads to choose a yellow Labrador. Liz especially regarded Shandy as a sort of live cuddly toy/human baby. He was stuffed with unsuitable food. While provided with expensive belongings galore, he was also underexercised and bored. Henry had strict instructions to keep Shandy on a lead always and to avoid contact with other dogs.

One day, during his usual brief stroll for toilet purposes, Shandy, overcome by the interesting smell of a female, slipped his collar and shot off. Henry searched the neighborhood in vain.

A panic-stricken Liz contacted the police, the lost dogs' home, and the local radio station, offering a generous reward. She was thoroughly relieved when a small boy appeared leading a mud-covered smelly Labrador on a piece of string. She willingly handed over the promised cash before giving the dog a huge meal. After such a horrific experience, she decided the best place for Shandy to recover would be in the comfort of the master bedroom, and the very necessary bath could wait. When a leg-weary but relieved Henry returned, he was forbidden to disturb the snoring mound under the bedclothes.

However, not long afterward, an irate Labrador owner turned up with the genuine Shandy in tow. They had the wrong Labrador cozily tucked up in their king-size bed, and doting Liz at least was quite unaware of it.

As long as somebody benefits by a mistake, all is not lost.

🏠 A Fortuitous Moment

by Edy Makariw

I 'D JUST GOTTEN my first paycheck in years, and I wanted to celebrate. But my partner was away visiting relatives and I really didn't want to come home alone to a dark, empty house.

So, where should I wind up but at the pet supply store? And why should I happen to notice that tiny black animal asleep, looking so much like our black cat, just recently lost to cancer? And how is it that the owner of the store, Jerry, happened to open up that cage and gently lift that little black puppy out and hold it toward me?

Ten years later, I sometimes still wonder why, rather than politely pushing him away, I reached forward and took hold of that little pup and held him tight.

That still-drowsy creature sniffed at my coat collar, licked my chin, and then laid his tiny jaw on my forearm and went back to sleep with a contented sigh. After I'd held him for a little while, I knew it was right for me to go home to my dark, empty house, for now, I had a bright, filled spirit within me. As I went, I realized that many other folks on the same schedule that my partner and I keep, in the same kind of small house, are able to have relationships with well-behaved dogs that are just as large as that little lab-shepherd mix would likely become one day.

Why, of all times, did Jerry close shop early on that evening when I went back to bring *my* dog home?

∞ *Awakenings happen when and where they will. A positive attitude helps. You never know what it is that will trigger you into understanding something you never realized before.*

··

⌂ Drndl Doggl Longs for Hollywood

by Theresa Mancuso

MIDWAY THROUGH MY seven years as a nun at New Skete, the monks decided, or so Brother Peter told me, that since I had a natural propensity for spoiling puppies, I was just the right person to take care of a German shepherd named Drndl Doggl. My job was to boost his deficient self-confidence and fuss with his dietary needs until he recovered sufficiently for adoption.

I advanced Drndl Doggl's inner man by initiating him into the delights of acting. I costumed the canine boy in various modes of apparel, improvising with materials found in the monastery upholstery shop or among castoff garments that would eventually make their way to a charity clothing bin. The dog became obsessed with dreams of stardom. Drndl Doggl wanted Hollywood.

He launched his bid for a movie career in the back yard of the monastery—not an auspicious beginning, but who could tell that to a headstrong pup? I made a slide show of Drndl Doggl in costume with the theme music from *Masterpiece Theater* as background. He paraded in artistic array, trying on the parts he longed to play on stage or in film, dressed like Mohammed Ali, Cardinal Richelieu, and Audie Murphy in *The Red Bad of Courage.*

When it was time for Drndl Doggl to leave the monastery for his new home, he wasn't moving to Hollywood, but eastward to Connecticut. I resisted his pleading and my own urge to advance his movie career instead by finding him a good agent.

∞ *Self-confidence increases every time we measure up to our own standards as well as those of others. Creative cooperation with circumstances is often the key to success.*

⌂ What Fools These Mortals Be

by Dr. Nancy Bekaert

I MET MY FIRST AIREDALE after more than fifteen years as a professional dog trainer. I was captivated by this breed's complete lack of decorum. In my youthful conceit, I was determined to do what no other trainer seemed able to do—train an Airedale to perform with military precision.

For months we struggled, until finally, bruised and battle weary, I emerged victorious . . . or so I thought. The day arrived.

Contenders gathered. There was time for one last practice. He snapped to a heel and stayed in tight. He dropped on recall and remained until a nod brought him to a polished finish. Yes! We were ready!

The moment came, and we stepped into the ring.

"Forward," said the judge.

"Heel," I commanded, and strode confidently across the ring.

"About turn," the judge directed. I turned. There was Loxley, tail wagging, bouncing along the fence line greeting the spectators. I glared and continued forward. Loxley smiled as he passed me going in the opposite direction.

He shook "paws" with the judge while standing for exam, "played dead" during the recall, "begged" for most of the long sit, and ended the long down with a "GI-Joe crawl" across the ring.

"Not good enough to pass," said the judge as she patted my shoulder, "but he certainly was the most entertaining dog I've ever judged."

∞ *Getting the last word is an irresistible urge!*

⌂ You Never Know

by Louise Maguire

C INDY, MY COLLIE CROSS, was two when Juli, her six-week-old half-sister, joined our household. Cindy had been my private dog since she was nine months old, passed on to me because she had become increasingly jealous of her mother. I hoped that Cindy would accept a puppy, so I made various house rules beforehand to keep her happy in top-dog position.

A barrier would hold Juli in the kitchen while I was out, leaving Cindy the rest of the house. Like Juli, Cindy would enjoy four meals a day. Cindy would keep sleeping privileges on my bed, while Juli would sleep in a basket on floor level.

The first meeting went off so easily that I wondered if Cindy realized they were sisters. Juli loved Cindy's company from the beginning. If I left them shut apart, on my return, they would greet me with two eager faces and tails wagging, side by side. The kitchen barrier was useless. Juli quickly learned to scale it.

Cindy never objected to Juli's company, and Juli foiled my every attempt to divide them. The basket on the floor didn't last. I woke one morning to find Juli curled in the crook of my arm and Cindy, tucked up at the end of the bed.

∞ *You never know how things will turn out.*
....

⌂ My Dog Is Cuter Than Me

by Scott Cohen

GOD LAUGHED when He made Wilson. Wilson has prominent black eyes that act like bumpers when he's exploring. A tooth or two protruding from his lower lip punctuates a short snout. When Wilson walks, his tail wags so vigorously it sometimes knocks him over, and when he runs, his large ears make him look like he may take off any minute.

Taking Wilson out is an adventure. He's not too keen on other dogs, but he does love people. Girls disengage from their boyfriends to rush over to him.

Guys say, "Man, that dog is so cute, he's a babe magnet."

Whenever we come in from a walk, Wilson runs behind the desk to greet the doorman. Toddlers who see him exclaim, "Doggie! Mommy, look at that doggie." The modest Wilson takes it all in stride. Smiling, he places his whole head in the hand that reaches down to pat him.

In a video store one day, we were playing hide-and-seek between the aisles when Willie noticed a three-year-old in a stroller. He strode up and dropped down beside her. The girl giggled and petted him, to her father's amazement. "She's terrified of dogs," he said.

Wilson's a quiet dog, but one time he ran between the legs of a group of rumbling teenagers. He let out a series of clipped barks and distracted them so that they stopped fighting and started petting him.

"Can we pick him up, Mister? He's so cute, what kind is he?"

∞ *Anyone who spreads joy will be loved and valued wherever he or she goes.*

⌂ Ugly in the Hospital

by Gail Smart

UGLY WAS IN the hospital again. My white boxer seems to spend more time seeing specialists than he does at home. This time he had been away for a week with major jaw surgery at a plush animal hospital near Cambridge, in England.

I waited for my turn while the man in front collected his beautiful young Weimaraner bitch. She came through the doors, screaming with delight as soon as she saw her owner. I heard the attendants tell him that she had been terribly depressed, clearly pining for home. You can't explain to dogs that you'll soon be back for them.

Next it was my turn, and Ugly came swinging along happily with his nurse. As they approached, he looked up at my face, smiled in recognition, and passed me by on his way toward the exercise pen, seeming to say, "Shan't be long—just going out with my nurse."

The nurse had to stop him and bring him back. She pretended he hadn't seen me, assuming I would be hurt.

Once returned to me, Ugly happily jumped into our car. The nurses didn't have to say this dog was a sad chap pining for home. Instead, they reported that he always greeted them with joy and happily joined in every activity. It's hard to imagine a dog more easygoing or a better patient.

∞ *Even tough stuff like being sick can be an opportunity to meet new people and spread a little happiness.*

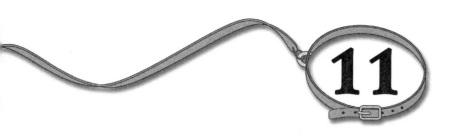

Go Fetch:
Starting over Again, Every Day of Your Life

DOGS WILL CHASE A BALL or stick in endless repetition, never tiring, never giving up. They rise to the occasion every time we give the command, "Go fetch." Even when they're dog-tired, lying down and spent, or even completely asleep, if you pick up a ball or a stick or one of their favorite toys, and poise to pitch it, dogs will fly after the desired object. A dog with sound temperament never gives up.

Dogs can overcome incredible obstacles and remain resilient in the face of difficulties. They will swim or run at breakneck speed, forcing themselves to keep on going with an eye on the prize. The thing with dogs is that every day's a new beginning. How could we ever doubt that from them, we might finally learn to do it right, no matter what it takes?

Many times we are forced to garner some inner drive deep within ourselves in order to face life's challenges. Starting over again is one of the hardest challenges we face in life. I learned that lesson more than twenty years ago, and I try never to forget it. I was forty-one years old when I left the monastery after being in religious community life for twenty-two years. I had never had to earn a living or create a home of my own before. I came to appreciate early on how much canine friends teach us and how much they give while asking little in return. Go fetch! Indeed, face the challenges that await you. Overcome them. Get up and start again; never lose heart. Make a new beginning every time you must; do not quit and do not be afraid.

"Life is for you all the way," Sister Diane told me one day when I was starting out my monastery life at New Skete. I played that tape in my mind many times. Let each day be a new beginning, fresh and clean. Leave the baggage of the past behind you. Strive to become the person you were meant to be, for it's never too late to start again.

⌂ Homecoming

by Scott Cohen

I WAS A NEW DOG OWNER fresh out of rehab, where I had learned the value of structure. It's generally not recommended to adopt a pet in early recovery, but I was lonely and felt that my addiction had kept me from accepting normal adult responsibilities. I was determined.

I carefully researched dogs, and began at once to prepare a "nest." Dogs, the manuals claimed, feel most secure in small soft places. My experiences had taught me all about the value of security.

I set up the kitchen with a gate, several blankets, and water and food bowls, and I placed my new friend in his makeshift kennel.

In bed, I'd just begun my devotional readings, when a single paw and then another came over the side of the mattress. Next, a full canine face was breathing hotly on my cheek. He had climbed the gate.

"Do you wanna' come up, boy?" I asked, beginning the one-sided dialogue that is the mark of the devoted pet-owner. All at once I was engulfed in a hot panting cloud of intemperate affection and gratitude. After a diffident sniff at the book I was reading, two three-hundred-and-sixty-degree surveys of his chosen nest, a final scratch behind his ears, and a loud canine yawn, my new friend was fast asleep. I turned off the light with the serene reflection that my first day's training had been a success. From the foot of the bed my dog's soft snores sounded like agreement.

∾ Starting over whenever you need to is the most important decision you'll ever make. The support and encouragement of unswerving companionship is helpful.

....

⌂ Journey Together Forever

by Peter Landy

M Y KINSHIP WITH DOGS began in Transylvania, my birthplace. Underneath my baby crib sat a watchful terrier mix named Bobbi. She became my shadow and best friend. Many years later, it was Hansel's turn. Of his twelve littermates, Hansel (Hans) exhibited the most bravado, so I selected him and destiny joined our paths.

After my mom passed away and our home was sold, my uncle insisted that Hans was holding me back from my career and had to go. I put my uncle out of my life instead. Hans and I pulled up our roots and headed north into the Catskills to our mountain hideaway, a rustic cabin without heat, water, or lavatory. By a stroke of luck at the twenty-third hour, we found a place to live on a working 300-acre dairy farm near Cobbleskill. The owner had 150 Holstein cows, several draft horses, and two dogs.

When I found a new job in Albany, I found a small cottage with no pet restrictions, and we settled in. My new job was going well, but I often had overnight assignments, so Hans accompanied me on business trips to anywhere from Long

Island to Canada until spinal degeneration paralyzed him. It was time for our last journey to the veterinarian. Hans laid his head on my foot as the sleeping serum took effect, exchanging Earth for heaven where I could not follow. It was not yet my time, but my heart will be with him forever.

∞ *New beginnings can be portals to happiness. It's easier if you take along a companion.*

....

🏠 The Story of Nexus, a Guide Dog

by Dory Bartell

I GOT MY FIRST GUIDE DOG in May of 1996, a black Lab named Nexus. We were a team for eighteen months until tragedy struck.

One afternoon, soon after I returned from the hospital after back surgery, I went out with Nexus to get the mail. A neighbor's dog suddenly attacked her with no provocation and chewed her from neck to tail. In my weakened state, I was unable to help my dog, though I tried and further injured my back doing so. I screamed for help and finally, the neighbor who owned the Dalmatian came over and called off her dog.

We rushed Nexus to the vet, where her injuries were taken care of. The vet would not take any money for the service. The owners of the Dalmatian did not feel they needed to do anything since she was "just a dog."

We hired an attorney and took them to court. Animal control had a "dangerous dog" hearing and the Dalmatian was put down, but not before it bit several children. We won our legal battle after a two-year struggle with their insurance company, but Nexus had to be retired from guide dog service because she would no longer work in harness. She is enjoying retirement as queen of the house and does dog therapy at the hospital, accompanying us whenever we can take her along with my new Labrador guide, Campbell.

∞ Starting over again after tragedy destroys what you have begun demands extraordinary courage and determination.

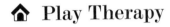 ## Play Therapy

by Irene Smith

WHEN THEY BROUGHT Rio to us, he was profoundly depressed. A beautiful two-year-old pedigreed German shepherd, this dog had been terribly abused. His eyes were deep pools of despair. Rio took up residence in the coat closet and refused to eat. While he consented to be walked, he shuffled like an old man. We took turns sitting in front of the closet and talking softly to him. He listened gravely and finally deigned to take treats of cheese and chicken from our hands. Still, though, he declined to participate in the life of the household.

One cold February night about two weeks after his arrival, I walked Rio and Haiku, a four-month-old Shepherd mix pup, up to the dead end of the street and let them off their leashes in a big fenced lot. There was a layer of new snow on the ground. Haiku streaked off, circled the perimeter of the lot and came back to run rings around Rio, inviting him to play. Rio watched for a few minutes, seemingly without interest, sitting listlessly in the snow.

Finally, Rio stood up, shook himself vigorously, and started to run. Haiku, delighted, followed him. I stood in the snow until my feet were blocks of ice watching them. They ran, they rolled, they turned somersaults, they leaped, they danced, they had mock wrestling matches. In Haiku there was the infinite energy of a puppy; in Rio, the look of a prisoner finally let out of his terrible jail. Life was starting over for Rio.

∞ *Never forget how to play. It will keep you young and happy no matter how many times you have to start your life all over again.*

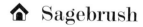 Sagebrush

by Gary Stafford

THIS IS A STORY ABOUT a little brindle pit bull. She was malnourished and still nursing a five-month-old puppy when animal control found her wandering the streets in a small Maine town. They put her into a shelter kennel along with her pup where she snarled at everyone who approached her. My wife, Terri, went in to see her when animal control called her for a consultation. Terri suggested that they put the puppy in another room and keep them separated, so the mother's milk would dry up. The shelter eventually found the owner, who didn't want her back. Rage, as she had been called, was used only for breeding anyway, and they didn't want to pay for boarding and shots.

The poor dog only weighed thirty-five pounds, but her temperament was really great once she was no longer afraid for or protective of her puppy. She was spayed and joined our household as Sagebrush. After minimal training, she even joined our other dog, Hilda, as a therapy dog, entertaining children on holidays, even wearing costumes that my wife made. Nursing home residents loved her because of her quiet, gentle ways. Sage bonded with me even more than with Terri and spent her free time crawling into my lap whenever I sat down to read the paper. We've had her for many years now and I believe she must be thirteen years old. Sagebrush is retired and matron of all our dogs.

∞ *Given half a chance and properly understood, anger can be exchanged for gentleness and compassion.*

218   *Dog People Do It Better*

⌂ Knowing What Makes You Tick

by Theresa Mancuso

I HAD NO DOG OF MY OWN when I rescued a German shepherd mix from just outside the gate at the Brooklyn Botanical Garden. I lifted his frail and bony body into my car and gently removed more than a hundred ticks from his starving frame. He never made a single sound, just lay there on the car seat as if he were about to breathe his last, thankful to be with someone who cared.

I brought the stray home and made my way stealthily through the front door, hoping that my landlady would not descend the front steps and find me sneaking a canine into her fortress. We went first to the bathroom, where I gently finished the great cleanup he so badly needed. Then I made dinner for him, perhaps the only meal he had taken for weeks. My only pet was a small Siamese cat, who took the stray dog under her wing, so to speak, bopping him on the nose as he grew playful once his hunger was satisfied and his body no longer ached or bled from tick bites.

Alas, my landlady caught up with me sometime during the first week and delivered her ultimatum. It was the dog or both of us—out the door! I prevailed upon her tender heart to let him remain until I could find a proper home for him. The young family that promised to love him for the rest of his life called him "Lucky" and why not? He surely was.

∞ *Most of us would do well to face our lives as strays do, without*

a whimper or complaint, but ever able to start over given half
a chance.
....

🏠 The Magic Milk Mixture

by Irene Smith

W HEN THE POLICE CAR stopped in front of my house,
I knew I wasn't in trouble with the law. The compassion-
ate cops of NYPD's Twenty-Fifth Precinct were bringing me
some woebegone little critter they had found. This was a puppy
they had pulled out of a trash basket, a skeletal little ice cube,
breathing but close to death, maybe seven weeks old.

We *hate* to see babies die. In two decades of animal rescue
work in East Harlem, we have become experts at bringing baby
creatures back from the brink. Our secret weapon for puppies
is something we call the Magic Milk Mixture. Take two cups of
whole milk, fortify with two tablespoons of powdered milk,
mix in a blender with an egg and one teaspoon of brewer's
yeast. Let the puppy drink as much as he wants, but stop for a
day or two if he develops diarrhea. Supplement with a good
brand of puppy chow. Always provide a generous supply of
fresh water.

Nicodemus was typical of most of the starving pups we
put on our regimen. He began to gain weight, and at two
weeks his rickets began to disappear and his bones were
stronger. In another two weeks he had started to look and

act like a normal puppy.

Nicodemus turned out to be an Irish wolfhound, the size of a small pony. He is living happily ever after on four fenced-in acres in New Jersey with his very own teenage boy.

∞ *Everybody needs to create for themselves a spiritual Magic Milk Mixture, the right combination of silence, reflection, and prayer added to relaxation and fun to restore them from the frazzling of life.*

....

🏠 Letting Go

by Bridgette Mongeon

MY OLD DOG TOOK ILL. That week was a swarm of emotions. Conan's stomach had turned, which I hear is common in large dogs. Surgery was immediate. When we brought the dog in to the emergency room, they tried to get me to leave him. "You will have to cut my wife's arms off, to get her to let go of this dog," my husband informed the technician. He let me stay for the exam.

After surgery, I begged them to let me see my dog. An IV was hooked up to his leg, and because he was so large they laid him on the floor for recovery. I snuggled up to his back, and pretended to be invisible.

Later the doctor told me that his vital signs improved when I was there so they decided to let me stay through the night.

There was nothing else that they could do. We brought Conan home, laid him on his orange rug in the kitchen, and hung the IV on the dishwasher.

It had been days of trauma for the family. Once again I snuggled behind Conan, this time falling asleep in exhaustion. My husband stayed in front of him. As I slept Conan passed away. I was mortified. "Why?" I cried "Why couldn't I be awake when he passed?" My husband simply said. "I could see his eyes, every time you spoke to him he would struggle to live. You needed to be asleep so he could go."

∞ *Change comes whether we are ready for it or not. Great love will see us through.*
....

🏠 A Home of Her Own

by Lee Hough

A LICE WAS GERMAN shepherd royalty, for her father won the National Working Championship in Germany. She had earned Schutzhund titles and was approved for breeding. Alice had two pups by an accidental breeding and the trainer only shrugged when just one survived. He was annoyed that his prize bitch had been bred accidentally.

Alice remained kenneled. Then she was bred and shipped elsewhere to whelp her litter. I asked to buy her, but the trainer rebuffed me. She was too valuable for breeding.

Later, I learned that several dogs had died in his kennel and there were repercussions. Training ended. Alice returned from having her litter and went back into the kennel. I offered yet again to take her and another female, but they were fertile, so her trainer refused.

A year passed, and another dog died. The trainer failed to appear for a court hearing and the authorities decided to euthanize his remaining dogs because they had "attack training." Poor Alice. An e-mail came: "Will someone come and get these dogs?"

So Alice finally came home with me. She had a litter in my living room. Happily sleeping upside down on the couch or riding in the front seat of my pickup truck, Alice is content now with a home and family, other dogs and a person of her own. Her son will carry on her excellent lines and her daughters have good homes. Every dog deserves a soft bed and a loving home.

∞ *Even if it takes a long time to make the right thing happen, never give up trying.*
....

⌂ Geisty Tells All

by Theresa Mancuso

I ALWAYS SAID THAT IF I ever wrote my autobiography, the title would have to be *Dog Hairs and Dust* since I've never been able to rid my life of this irksome combination brought about by the presence of my three German shepherd dogs and the cats they hang out with. So when I clean house, I do so with a passion.

A few years back, several good friends prevailed upon me to speak with an animal communicator. Skeptically, I contacted Marlene. Within several moments of her first session with Geisty, Marlene was finding out things that only the animals in my household and I could really know. She told me that Geisty would prefer it if I were to wash the dogs' bowls after every meal, rather than simply letting them lick the bowls clean.

And then, as if impelled to do so for integrity's sake but not wishing to hurt my feelings, Marlene continued, "Oh, yes, and Geisty also said that they [meaning the animals] like the place to be *moderately* clean."

"What's that supposed to mean?" I asked.

"It means," Marlene responded, "at least according to Geisty, that the animals don't like it when you get all in a frenzy cleaning house. It makes them nervous to see you rushing around wildly sweeping, dusting, vacuuming, and mopping floors. You just get too hyper. Geisty said they like it better when you're calm and relaxed, even if the house isn't as clean as you want it to be."

What can you do with a dog that tells all?

∞ *Regular household routines remind us that every day should be a new beginning.*

⌂ Kalli Bear

by Terri J. Stafford

W E WERE GOING Christmas shopping, but as we drove past the local animal shelter, I told my boys I wanted to stop in and see what was there. We heard the most awful barking out back, and there in a pen we found a black-brindle pit bull terrier that didn't look very good. She responded positively as I looked her over. I saw that she had many sores underneath her thin coat and she definitely needed some weight put on her. I filled out the paperwork and off we went shopping.

Later that day, we came back to pick up our newly adopted dog, and there we heard her short but awful story. Someone had tied this dog to a lamppost in a store parking lot after beating her mercilessly. She was left tied in the bitterly cold December night and found the next morning. After months of veterinary visits and medication, lots of good food, and plenty of love and patience, Kalli Bear, as we called her, finally settled down. She grew in confidence and became a rambunctious five-year-old with a mind of her own. Kalli loves to play ball and will run and fetch anything you can throw. Her favorite job is moving water from one place to another by digging rivers and watching the water run. Kalli Bear has always distrusted people she doesn't know, but never bites, choosing to leave the room instead. She's eleven years old now, and we don't regret a single day of having her in our family.

∞ *The ability to overcome obstacles is a hallmark of strong character.*

⌂ Dr. Chablis

by Lori Sash-Gail

CHABLIS IS NOT JUST an elegant, immaculately groomed fluff of a dog—she holds a serious occupation at St. Vincent's Hospital in New York as an animal-assisted activity dog, for which she has received two certifications.

One day, the nurses requested that Chablis make a special visit to a police officer who had been shot in the head. We entered the room, and I put Chablis on the officer's lap. He responded immediately with much excited blinking and eye movements. Then Chablis made her way up to the officer's face and licked his lips. He took hold of her leash, pursed his lips, and kissed her back. Police officers in full uniform stood by and encouraged their buddy, "Ah," they said, "you've got a new girl-friend!" There were lots of smiles and cheers. When it was time to leave, the patient held Chablis' leash tightly between his thumb and index finger and refused to let her go.

The next morning, the officer spoke his first words in three months: "I had a little white poodle come in here and visit me yesterday," he said to his mother. Three days later he was discharged to a rehabilitation center and is now at home. Later, we found out that Chablis' picture is posted at the precinct and she is known as the dog who made their buddy speak.

∞ More miracles happen because of love than this world dreams of! Hold fast to love; it is the heart's survival gear.

♠ The Good, the Bad, and Ozark

by Mary Frenzel-Berra

OZARK WAS AN ADULT bloodhound adopted from the ASPCA to be my guard dog for a four-month period while my husband was away doing fieldwork. I planned to pretend the ninety-pound bloodhound was mean and refused to let him be petted or fussed over when we walked around the neighborhood. My prior dog had been small, cute, and cuddly, so she'd never looked the part.

When I brought Ozark home, our six-pound cat batted him into the bathroom and wouldn't let him out. The cat would stretch out languidly in front of Ozark's food, something she had never done to our other dog because she knew better. He couldn't eat until I saved him.

Ozark *looked* tough with his huge red-rimmed eyes and bloodhound drool. His bark, though rarely used, was formidable. But Ozark adored people. He radiated friendliness, but, as planned, I did not allow him to be petted. When he rolled over for a tummy rub from strangers, I dissuaded him. Clearly disappointed, Ozark tried even harder to connect with people.

After four months, Bob returned home, and I was no longer the only occupant in our fourteen-story building as students started arriving and taking up residence in the apartments. I no longer needed protection. I took Ozark to Ironton, Missouri, and rehomed him with a family there. Months later, a man stopped me in the street and commented that Ozark was a wonderful dog. I wished that I had given Ozark a chance to meet and greet his admirers all along.

∞ *For every plan, there is a consequence, not necessarily an intended one.*
....

⌂ Baby Blue

by Catherine Raven Feher-Elston

I WAS IN LAME DEER, Montana, when a scrawny, starving puppy walked up to me. I could count every one of her ribs. Her hipbones protruded, she was covered with sores, and she was smelly—the legacy of a nasty case of mange. She had the markings of a German shepherd, the perky ears of a husky, and gigantic paws. Clear evidence of her Arctic legacy was a beautiful blue eye. The other was brown.

She accepted food and water gratefully. I knew she'd die within a few days unless she received help immediately. I took her into my arms and placed her in the van, saying, "I'll take care of you now, Baby Blue."

On arriving home, I prepared a bed and a tarp covering for Baby Blue. I fed her three times daily to help her achieve a healthy weight. I traveled twenty miles to get her puppy shots and antimange injections. I didn't let her near my own dogs, for fear of contagion, but they knew she was there.

After two weeks, I arranged for ten days of intensive treatment with a vet. This dog looked about three months old, but turned out to be six months old. Her growth had been stunted by malnutrition. Baby Blue gained twelve pounds.

Today she's a healthy, happy, and disease-free puppy adored by Denali, my malamute, and Aurora, my wolf.

∞ *It takes great determination to save a being from the jaws of death.*
....

⌂ Wrongly Accused

by Ali Moore

SPARKY WAS MISUNDERSTOOD. The English bulldog and her human neighbor had been friends for years, but suddenly, one day, allegedly, she jumped up and bit him on the chin. The fact is that Sparky hadn't bitten him at all! It was all a mistake! Unable to protest her innocence, Sparky was impounded by animal control and there she stayed, frightened and alone, for ten long days. Her former owners decided that she had become too much of a liability and contacted me and Bulldawg Rescue for help. I agreed to take Sparky after her quarantine.

When I met Sparky, I truly doubted her intentions toward her former neighbor. Her two-inch underbite spoke volumes. Her lower teeth were completely exposed! When she introduced herself to us with kisses, I could feel her lower teeth scraping my face. That evening when my husband came home from work, Sparky eagerly ran to greet him. She jumped up with her tongue out to kiss him, but wound up nicking him on the chin with her bottom teeth. No bite intended!

After a month in rescue, Noel and Kristin came along. I told them about her record and they opened their hearts and home. Over the years Noel and Kristin have reported that friends and coworkers adore Sparky. In fact, she has such good public relations skills that she has become the unofficial mascot of the local university's romance languages department. Case closed!

∞ *Never judge without examining all aspects of the case.*

🏠 Successful Doggy Diet

by Paul Sutton

H AVE YOU EVER had to put your dog on a diet? Last year I had three rather overweight Border collies doing agility, knocking jumps, flying in all directions. It was very frustrating to say the least. When someone tactfully mentioned that it might be due to the few extra pounds they might be carrying, I decided to put all three of them on a diet. I had tried it in the past, but their woeful expressions when they saw their half rations was always just too much to bear, so out came the treats!

However, this time has been so different. Instead of cutting them back, I devised a diet of vegetables, rice, and ground turkey, plus half their normal ration of kibble. What a triumph! They love it and have a good bowlful of food. In a year, they have all lost about eleven pounds each and look so much better for it. To prove it was the weight causing the problem, Summer, this year, has achieved twenty-two clear rounds at agility, success at every show we have entered, when she only had four clears last year. Sunny has managed his first ever clear rounds over two-and-a-half-foot jumps and has clocked up five of them this year. Whisper has five clear rounds in her veteran class—clear every time. I just wish I was as successful with my own diet—bring on the veggies and rice!

∞ *Each day's another day to eat right and keep healthy. Keep on trying.*

⌂ Dog Eaters No More

by Theresa Mancuso

TO ACCOMMODATE RESIDENTS of my co-op building who might not have enjoyed my dogs as much as I did, I complied with house rules and generally held to an even higher standard wherever possible. Nevertheless, one day after I had lived there for a few years, one of my neighbors, a middle-aged man of foreign descent, accosted me.

"What is there about you, a nice lady like you seem to be, gentle and serene, yet you have to have these killer dogs living with you?" he asked. My three German shepherds stood by wagging their tales and smiling doggie smiles.

"They're *not* killer dogs," I answered.

"They look like wolves," he said. "Aren't you afraid they'll turn on you and kill you?" He smiled as if he liked the idea.

"Not at all," I responded. "Your children will kill you before my dogs ever turn on me. You read about kids murdering their parents all the time."

"In *my* country," the man said with almost a growl in his voice, "we *eat* dogs."

A few years later, the man and his wife purchased a long, low-cut dachshund, a hot dog of sorts, but I guess by that time they were dog-eaters no more.

∞ *No matter how hard you try, there will always be people who are dead set against you for reasons of their own, which you may never know. The best you can do is try and try and try again to meet them on their own terms, and when you can't manage that, it's time to walk away.*

⌂ Denali, the Great One

by Catherine Raven Feher-Elston

WHILE I WAS LIVING in Austin, Texas, a medicine man from Old Crow, Yukon, contacted me. He said that the village children had learned about a death I had been grieving and they were praying to help me be strong.

"Someone is coming to you," he explained. A few days later, a woman from a kennel near Houston told me to check for a red dog with Cascade Kennels in Washington State. I contacted Cascade. They said they didn't have any red pups but would keep in touch. A few more days later they called me about two red males, grandsons of their champion sled dog, Grizzly. "We were keeping them for ourselves, but thought you might want one. Come on up and choose the one you want, if you decide to take one," Madeleine offered.

By the first of November, I was in Washougal. I opened a big barn door and out raced two roly-poly red bundles. One brother reached me first and proceeded nibbling on my toes.

"Oh, it's you," I cried. "Here he is, Red Denali, Denali Shondeen." In Athabascan, *Denali* means "the Great One." She is a goddess personified in the great Mountain of the North, Denali, called Mt. McKinley by the whites. *Shondeen* is Dineh for "Sunshine." Denali is my sunshine. He brought joy and hope back into my life, and helped heal the wounds and pain of the past for Aurora and myself.

∞ *Miracles await us around every corner, beside every turn. Hold fast to faith and move forward with your life.*

Come, Fido:
All This and Heaven, Too

HAVING A BELOVED DOG such as those described in this book makes human life so complete, who could ask for more? According to my faith, God calls each of us into being, and then when our time on earth is done, God calls us again—by name—unto Himself. Not all readers will share this belief. Nevertheless, everyone who has loved a dog knows the joy and fulfillment that is felt every time we call that cherished pet, "Come, Fido," and know the approach of one who greets us with such unconditional love.

Certain aspects of our relationship with dogs invite us to greater awareness, deeper comprehension, and more profound engagement with the natural universe. Dogs take us to the brink—to the place where we define ourselves as persons of integrity, commitment, and dedication. Perhaps, the brink is where we are tested, where our deepest, most heartfelt convictions are challenged. Perhaps, the brink is where time meets eternity and life meets destiny, the place where earth and heaven come together just within our grasp.

These anecdotes suggest reflective moments in which we might ponder, not just the things we think we understand but, most of all, those we don't, the things that trouble us because they elude our control and comprehension. Striving to look more deeply into reality, we must first accept in humble awareness all of our own personal limitations and those of the times and cultures from which we come. Only then can we know the power of words that tell us to come forth to a new place of gentleness, awareness, and completion.

⌂ Carving a Memory

by Bridgette Mongeon

I WAS LUCKY to have one of those absolutely incredible dogs. Conan, a black Labrador retriever/collie mix was smart and loving and the best birthday present I had ever received. We had great experiences together through many years and losing him was extremely difficult.

Not long after his death, my husband came into my sculpture studio and found me sobbing, sculpting Conan.

"If it hurts so much, then why are you doing it?" he asked.

"Because I have to," I replied between sobs. The sculpture was of Conan lying on the ground and me snuggled up to his back. A memory filled with emotion, that I had captured in clay.

I put photos of the sculpture into my portfolio. Later on, as I worked on a commissioned sculpture of two small children, their mother saw the sculpture of Conan and reminisced about their own old Lab that they knew wouldn't live much longer. I told them I would add the dog to the sculpture of the children at no cost.

One commission has lead into another, and now I regularly share the union of master and pet. As I capture memories for other pet owners, I am reminded about the bond Conan and I had. It is the same love I feel between clients and their pets. Each pet commission seems to reunite me with Conan as I lovingly mix adoration and memory into the clay.

∞ *Take time to capture memories now. Carve them in your heart and let them rise as sweet salve and inspiration.*

⌂ The Loaf Lives on as the Queen of All That Is

by Dr. Sue Ann Lesser

AFTER TEN YEARS OF LIVING, The Loaf lost the use of her front legs and soon after became very weak behind. She gave me that look that dogs do when it's time to let them go. That night, Michael carried all hundred pounds of her upstairs so we could sleep together one last time. At around 3 A.M., she woke me by brushing her whiskers against my face. I knew she was saying we still had work to do together.

The next day, my classmate put her to sleep—I knew I could never do it myself. It was odd in that I didn't feel the cold rush of wind that usually accompanies a spirit being released from the body. The Loaf was still around.

About two months later, I was adjusting a litter of Doberman puppies, and a little black bitch with a pink ribbon around her neck reached up and brushed her whiskers against my face. I knew it was my Loaf come back.

When I brought the puppy home, she went right to the bed that Loaf had always slept in and lay down. She had the same way of "laughing" and that same big soft protective feel in bed. The Loaf's name is now Quila, and she has continued as my teacher. She has earned her UD (Utility Dog, the Ph.D. of competition obedience). I have used my knowledge of training Quila to the betterment of my patients and clients.

The spirit always lives.

∞ *Death is not the end, but only a passage from this dimension to another. Do not be surprised to experience "contact" with the departed spirit of someone you love. Welcome such a visit. It is a startling and marvelous gift.*

....

⌂ Midnight Caller

by Theresa Mancuso

I HAD BEEN road-working my dogs for many years. Gaiting dogs beside a slowly driven automobile is excellent exercise.

My friend Maxine was accompanying me with her two dogs. We were driving less than five miles an hour, eyes on the road and our dogs. Since the dogs were often overtaking us, circling the van, I thought it would be safer to get out of their reach by picking up speed and veering left. I thought they were far enough away.

Something made me stop and call for Geisty, who was suddenly out of sight. Max leapt from the van. Beneath it was my beloved Geisty with her leg broken. The vet wrapped the leg in a soft cast and treated Geisty for shock. She seemed to be fine a few hours later, but when the vet went to set her leg, he discovered that she had begun to bleed profusely internally. She died on the operating table from cardiogenic shock.

Marlene Sandler, our animal communicator, said that Geisty told her over and over again that she forgave me for everything. My grief and feeling of guilt was terrible. But three days later, some time around midnight, Geisty stood at my bedside. It was a dream, perhaps—or was it? I reached for her and called her name, "Geisty, Geisty," as I embraced her close to my heart. A few moments later she was gone. I will never forget those several moments at midnight when I held her in my arms as I could not do when she died.

∞ *There are many things we can never explain this side of eternity. Let them be whatever they are. Take the blessing, and be grateful.*
....

🏠 Somerset Reuben James

by Terri J. Stafford

OUR SEVEN-YEAR-OLD SON, Matthew, came home from the hospital after five months of intense chemotherapy for acute alymphoblastic leukemia. The doctors said that he could benefit mentally if he had a puppy for companionship. The following spring we looked at a litter of Brittany spaniels, and Matthew picked out a large male that had climbed out of the pen and come to him. Matthew called his dog Somerset Reuben James—Ben for short.

During Ben's first year, he and Matthew grew together and loved each other greatly. Ben was there to comfort Matthew when he was very sick. As Matthew grew fit and got more involved with school again, Ben was always there waiting for him to come home and play or go walking together after school before bedtime.

Time went by, and when Matthew got his driving permit, he said to Ben, "Wait until I get my license, and then I'll take you driving with me." But some months before Matthew got his driver's license, Ben was diagnosed with stomach cancer. Matthew cried into Ben's fur, knowing he would never be able to take Ben with him when he got his first set of wheels.

Matthew's final words to Ben were, "You were always there for me and you made me better when I was sick. Although we didn't get to go driving together, you won't be in any more pain now either. I love you, Ben. Go to sleep now." Ben was nine years old, and Matthew was sixteen.

∞ *Love and companionship with a beloved pet can be a determining factor in recovery.*

⌂ Henry Paves the Way

by Marlene Sandler*

A WONDERFUL MUTT named Henry was absolutely the governor of all that he saw, his indomitable spirit bigger than his little brown-and-white body. When Peggy, his person, invited me to talk with Henry, he said that she would do important work with another animal to heal her relationship with her mom. Peggy was mystified but remained open.

On a follow-up visit to the vet, Peggy and Henry met Sophie, an eleven-year-old dog grieving for her person, who had passed away. Henry went to Sophie's cage, and Peggy couldn't get him away from it. He had made a soul connection with her. Peggy and her husband, Humphrey, observed Henry's despair at leaving Sophie behind and adopted her.

Sophie was lovely but had many health problems. She lost her sight, hearing, and bladder control. Henry taught her where everything was. He put his body against hers to support her. Walking together, Henry slowed his pace to keep abreast of Sophie.

They had been told that Sophie would only last about six months, but four years passed before she became really frail and ill. While preparing for Sophie's passing, Henry had a heart attack and died suddenly. It devastated them. Their strong little tank of a dog, always so healthy, was gone. Peggy phoned frantically, but I already knew Henry had gone to prepare the way for Sophie and Peggy's mother. Two weeks later, first Sophie and then the mother passed away.

Ꮼ *Do not ask why this one passes and another remains behind. The destiny of each soul is between itself and its Maker.*

*Names and other details have been changed to protect Marlene's clients' confidentiality.

🏠 The Red Toyota

by Theresa Mancuso

I N THE 80S, I drove a red Toyota Tercel hatchback. My three
German shepherds and I made many car trips in it, perhaps
not impressive by most standards, but for my pack, they were
great adventures.

My friends John and Jane Olsson, in Skowhegan, Maine,
welcomed us warmly. The Olssons have a boarding kennel,
and as they also bred German shepherds at the time, three
dogs more made it all the merrier. My dogs loved tracking
among the pine trees, searching for tidbits of meat and other
treats I had left on a trail prepared earlier each day. It grew
cool enough at night to fire up the potbellied stove in the living room, and the dogs and I would settle down around the
stove after tramping the fields and woods.

Coming down from Maine one year, I stopped at a road-
side restaurant that had a huge parking lot. I pulled up and
parked the Tercel, and, minding my own business, I set about
letting the dogs out of the car. I noticed people looking our
way. When Cara Mia jumped out of the car, the folks who
were watching smiled broadly. When Grip followed, the people laughed. But when eight-month-old Geisty flew out behind
her dad, the folks just broke up into loud guffaws and bent
over laughing.

Who would have dreamed that a red Toyota, so small and
compact, could carry so comfortably this three-pack of German
shepherds? It seemed to amuse our audience to no end!

∞ The simple pleasures of life need not be impressive to create lasting memories. They are the stuff of which happiness is made, and when we have walked our final mile, all this and heaven, too, awaits us. Would we have ever thought ourselves worthy?

···

⌂ Juli, A Rare Spirit

by Louise Maguire

OUR DOGS ARE NOBLER than we are; they don't complain about their fate. Juli displayed such fortitude in her eight-month unsuccessful fight for life

When I realized that Juli was urinating more than was normal, my vet carried out various treatments, culminating in an operation to check for cancer. We celebrated her all-clear with a sponsored dog walk. The frequent urinating continued and more ominously, her face was whitening fast.

The veterinarian recommended a second opinion. Juli had always been a good patient, accepting surgery without a fight. Throughout the long battery of examinations and X rays by various strangers, she continued to show this trust, the same dog that terrorized tramps and burglars, quietly accepting her fate. Finally, another operation revealed that she did have cancer, an obscure variety, only diagnosed because the growth had spread. Two to four months left was the verdict.

We made the most of it. We photographed Juli even more in those last months than we had during her puppy days. We took walks galore to all of her favorite haunts. Food treats, as always, remained a high point in Juli's day. Although she gradually lost weight, she kept her appetite and her enthusiasm for life.

Two months later, Juli died, still uncomplaining and, with the help of my vet, with her teeth firmly clamped on her last doggie chew. She was only ten and a true heroine in adversity. I appreciate that rare spirit all the more as I consider how differently I would have reacted in similar circumstances.

∞ *Cultivate the ability to face adversity with a serene spirit by accepting the annoyances and disappointments of every day.*

🏠 Power: Conrad Kenya, C.D. (1982–1995)

by Mary Frenzel-Berra

B LACK, MALE, eight- to ten-week-old American cocker spaniel, that's what we wanted. We named "him" Conrad's Heart of Darkness. Skittering to the car with our four-month-old red-and-white female in tow, Bob burbled, "Come, Conrad." So, Conrad it was. Never Connie. Never Connie, not for thirteen years.

Conrad had a sense of decorum. The world and most things in it should behave. She included herself in that category and worked very hard at instilling this quality in those around her. A friend of mine called her Calvin in tribute to her serious nature. Queen Victoria's quip, "We are not amused," came to mind on fairly frequent occasions. She enforced her standards.

Growling and carrying on were not her method. She perfected The Look. It was highly effective.

At a tracking event when we were heeling up to the start line, we passed a parked car. Unbeknownst to me, that car had two German shepherds underneath it keeping cool, and that car was on Conrad's side. As we passed, they both charged out, teeth bared. I jumped four feet straight up. Conrad didn't even break stride. The Look was bestowed, a backward glance. I never saw two shepherds sit, cease, and desist so fast. I was wobbly, but Conrad, unflappable, just marched along.

Nothing ever fazed that dog. Nothing. She did her jobs consistently well with a minimum of fuss and bother, and she expected those around her to do likewise. It worked. Conrad's world shaped up.

∞ *Insist, be adamant; expect, demand that others be amazingly able. Don't rant and rave. That expends too much energy and is, basically, a diversion. Consistency counts. Assurance is power.*

⌂ Mowgli, Son of Raven

by Catherine Raven Feher-Elston

WHILE I WAS RECOVERING from a serious illness one January, a young man offered me a golden male wolf cub. Before bringing it home, I took the cub to a nearby pond, and we walked in the snow together. He sniffed a spot and suddenly, his ears perked up as he jumped and hopped high like a coyote. When he landed, he started digging.

"Where's the mouse?" I laughed. "You're a jumper like a little frog, like a Mowgli. Mowgli was the little boy raised by a wolf in Kipling's *Jungle Book*. You will be the little wolf raised by me." I hugged him and took him home that very day. He grew stronger and more beautiful daily, and my strength increased.

I have never loved anyone the way I loved Mowgli. When I lost him to a birth defect two years later, I waited to die myself. I believe Mowgli was the embodiment of Wolf Spirit. When I did the soul-release ceremony for him on the slopes of a mountain four days after his passing, the biggest storm in a century swept in as I placed the last grain of cornmeal on the spirit arrow, pointing the path east to Father Sun.

In his honor I wrote *Wolfsong: A Natural and Fabulous History of Wolves*. Through my work, Mowgli lives again. As a kachina, who came to walk with me for a brief time, Mowgli never died, but lives forever.

∞ *Great Spirit comes to us in many ways. We must learn to look and listen lest we fail to realize the Sacred Presence is always with us.*

⌂ Top Dog

by Louise Maguire

T HE BELL RANG, and Misty raced Pearl to the door. I fielded the spaniel efficiently. "What a beauty!" Misty offered both front paws but was firmly eased to floor level.

"How old is she?"

"Ten months. And getting wilder and wilder," admitted Pearl. "You're our final hope."

"From now on she earns her keep. My secret weapon." I rattled a tin. Misty pattered over for a tiny treat. "Misty, sit." She sat. "Good girl! You didn't tell me she would sit on command."

"Only if she's bribed."

"Not a bribe, a reward." Misty performed several times then I quietly clipped on a lead.

"Brilliant," said Pearl. "I have to grab her."

"Never hurry. You'll only wind her up." Misty tried to charge to the door. I relaxed into my chair. "Misty, sit." The game continued. Misty lunged toward the door whenever I moved.

"One very determined dog." I finally unclipped the lead. "No walk today, Misty."

Misty's eyes turned mournful. She sat. I clipped on the lead. Step by step we moved toward the door. Misty gained more sitting practice. I reached for the handle. Misty braced herself.

"Misty, wait." As the door opened Misty dived. I closed it before her astonished nose. "I'm top dog. I go through doors first," I explained. "Misty, wait." Misty finally backed away from the opening door and lay down.

Pearl stared, "I hope I find such patience."

"You will." And fifteen years later, Misty still rolls over to prove that I am top dog.

∞ *Bribed, rewarded, or not, doing the right thing is the best way to go.*
....

⌂ You Are My Eyes

by Theresa Mancuso

W HEN I FIRST met Campbell, he was out of harness, relaxing with his owner, Dory, for whom he is a beloved furry son and devoted guide dog. Dory had suggested that I meet Campbell "out of harness so he could play." I wondered why she stressed the "out of harness" part.

At the time, I didn't understand what she meant by that, but I agreed to meet her group and Campbell in Dory's hotel room. The handsome Labrador cavorted like a puppy, his beautiful large head and intelligent eyes winning my heart as did his friendliness and playful maneuvers. But the moment Dory put Campbell in his work harness, the dog's demeanor changed completely. He was all business now.

"Find the door, Campbell," Dory commanded in a soft voice, and without hesitation, Campbell led the way. "Take me to the curb, Campbell," Dory said as we exited the building. Her guide dog went directly to the curb and sat, not allowing her to go into the street where traffic flowed heavily. Answering each one of Dory's commands with perfect obedience that showed his awesome intelligence, Campbell did his work with the same enthusiasm as he had played out of harness; he was completely attentive to the task of being Dory's eyes as well as her heart. I choked back tears as I watched him work. *This* is indeed, a dog for all seasons!

∾ *Physical blindness is a rigorous challenge and human catastrophe, but not an unyielding tragedy for a courageous, strong-hearted person.*

⌂ My Border Collie Family

by Paul Sutton

WHISPER CAME INTO MY LIFE when I was very low. My previous dog, Kizzy, had just died of leukemia at thirteen years of age. I was so traumatized that I really didn't want another puppy, but I was persuaded to go and see a litter of Border collies near my home.

I fell immediately and unconditionally in love with Whisper, and she has been my savior on many occasions. She is so named because "Kizzy is only a Whisper away." Everyone has sad times in life. Each time I have cried into Whisper's fluffy neck, she has listened patiently to all my woes and licked away my tears. She really is my best friend in the world and I love every single hair on her body. She has been my support when Mum died and when my horse had to be put down, both within three months of each other in 1994. When my relationship broke up, Whisper was there for me. She has always been comfort and support.

But, life is not all doom and gloom! Whisper gave me my two other canine loves, Summer and Sunny, two of seven puppies she had in 1995. She was and still is the most fantastic Mum. Although now twelve years old, Whisper is still playful with them, chasing them on our daily walks and enjoying life to the full. My life would be desolate without my beloved Border collie family.

∞ *They come to us in many ways, our angels of mercy, often wrapped up in canine bodies with four paws and wagging tails.*

⌂ Believe It or Not!

by Theresa Mancuso

A FRIEND OF MINE ONCE TOLD ME that she had accompanied a friend of hers to a prominent psychic for a personal reading. She herself was a skeptic and did not intend to participate in any way beyond being present as a companion to the other woman. They took their places at a small table and sat comfortably opposite the psychic. Before beginning her reading of my friend's friend, the psychic asked, "Who is Anne?"

My friend looked startled and waited for the other woman to answer, but there was nothing forthcoming so she said, "Well . . . er . . . my mother's name was Anne."

"Yes," said the psychic, "and your mother passed a few years ago, didn't she?"

My friend nodded, not without apprehension.

The psychic smiled gently and said to her, "Well, there's a woman named Anne standing right behind your chair, and she said to tell you the dogs are with her on the other side. All of them." Then she went forward to address the concerns of the woman who was actually consulting her.

My friend and her mother had both been German shepherd breeders for many years, in fact, all of their lives. They loved their dogs exceedingly and had many of them living right in the home as family members. A skeptic no more!

∞ *Seeing is believing; hearing is, too. There are things in life that we can never hope to explain, but neither can we deny them. It's the better part of wisdom to let things be whatever they are without requiring explanations or proof.*

⌂ "A Good Dog Is an Island of Sanity in a Lost World"

by Anne Martindale

M Y COUSIN ONCE SAID, "When I die, I'm coming back as Anne's dog." Of course my dog gets the best; he's my link to sanity.

Let's face it: life sucks. The demons of civilization seem to get stronger every day. But then there are dogs.

Trevor demonstrated his superior wisdom even back in the days of the dog trainer who told me to be "the boss." On walks, I would unfailingly "boss" us into magic thickets from which escape was impossible without a machete, but this never happened when Trevor picked the route.

If I could live like my dog, I'd be completely content. To awaken spooned in with the pack, to bask in massage and kisses, to yawn, arise, and play, to have a nature walk or dig, run, get wet and muddy, head to the tub for a foot bath, eat, and most important of all, to nap the afternoon away. Ah, what a life! Wake up and repeat cycle. End with more play, and spoon in with the pack.

The sanest person I know walks on four feet. If I could follow the wisdom of my dog all the time, how happy I'd be. All I can do is take my unavoidable daily dose of civilization and concentrate on a speedy return to the influence of my dog.

∞ *Contentment is accepting your fate in life, such as it is. That is the better part of wisdom, and dogs possess it a hundredfold.*

⌂ The Dogs We Left Behind

by Anthony Jerone

M Y JOB IN THE ARMY was to train dogs for tunnel detection and scout duty. I was a point man in a dog-soldier team, and my dog's alertness was the only thing between eternity and me. In all my steps on the sands of Vietnamese beaches, there were many times when I could have stepped on a tunnel and gotten killed, had it not been for the incredible ability of Willy, a German shepherd trained to locate underground spaces and hidden caches. He saved untold American lives.

Willy was around two years old when we parted. I had walked point with him on the beaches of Vietnam, but GIs who had worked with dogs couldn't take them home afterward. The dogs were government property.

After I got home, I tried in every way possible to get my dog back. I wrote to the President of the United States, to congressmen and senators, to anybody I thought might help, but any personal ties Willy had with me were subject to military orders.

Eventually, after 1975, Willy was retired from the army and shipped stateside, where his new job was to do security work at a clothing store. It seemed too late to disrupt his life again and my circumstances had changed, also. But as long as I live, I will never forget the valor and dedication of that tunnel dog.

∞ *Valor is all about doing your duty with loyalty and dedication, regardless of the outcome.*

Conclusion

DOGS COME INTO OUR LIVES in many ways and for many reasons, but all of them have significance that might go unnoticed were it not for the awareness of those who look beyond appearances to the heart of things. I hope these anecdotes have given you some opportunity to see more than the external reality of our furry four-footed friends. If indeed, dog people actually do it better, it is only when they take the time and make the effort to look beyond appearances and go to the heart of the matter. Such contemplation of our true place in the universe serves to keep us humble and urges us to appreciate the life that is ours.

Dogs teach us without uttering a single word. They teach us by their very being, their natural unaffected sincerity, just by being dogs. If we could just be ourselves, we, too, would find the harmony and peace we long to embrace. The real journey in life is not about achieving material prosperity, worldly fame, or personal power, though these things feel good when we have them. Rather, the road we travel must bring us back to the true self, where we shall understand how blessed we really are. Our most important task, it seems to me, is to be just like our dogs: fully alive, completely awake, totally involved in life, watchful, vigilant, devoted, loyal, dedicated, sincere, open, and honest.

Why else are we so crazy about dogs, if not because they invite us to a high standard of being?

Contributors

Brenda and Geoff Abbott of Cheyenne, Wyoming, have raised, shown, trained, and raced Samoyeds since the early 1970s under the kennel name Kriskella. Brenda has edited and/or contributed to several dog books.

Peter Altschul lives in Washington, D.C., with his current guide dog, a black Lab named Gifford.

Joan Antelman is a lifelong animal lover. She lives in Manhattan with her cats, TomTom, Zelda, and Winston, all adopted from shelters.

Jackie E. Athey has had German shepherds for over twenty-five years. She now has a twelve-and-a-half-year-old dog that is paraplegic and an eight-year-old bitch.

Susan Babbitt resides in Arizona and is lucky to have and have had a host of wonderful animals to share life with.

Lynzie Bacchus, seventeen years old, has been racing and training sled dogs since the age of nine. She lives in Michigan.

Dory Bartell lives in Florida. She lost her sight in 1996.

Dr. Muriel Beerman, Brooklyn, New York, teaches physical education at one of the local high schools. She has owned and loved Labradors for better than thirty years.

Dr. Nancy Bekaert, a resident in upstate New York, has handled and trained dogs for over thirty years. She is the author of *Woof—The Dog's Guide to Training Difficult Owners* and *Understanding Pet Nutrition.*

Jolanta Benal and her partner live in Brooklyn, where they are overrun with dogs, cats, and books.

Joan Bolger lives in Brooklyn, New York, with her furry friend, Gino, the Pom.

Enid Coel lives in Brooklyn, New York, where she teaches English as a second language (ESL) to immigrant adults. She is the devoted mother of her human son, David, and numerous feline and canine kids, too, all of whom are rescues.

Scott Cohen is a perpetual student. On hiatus from studies as a psychotherapist, he works as a performance developer. His dog, Wilson, is the best therapist he knows.

Louis B. Colby lives in Newburyport, Massachusetts, where he was born eighty-two years ago. His father started the famous Colby line of American pit bull terriers in 1889. He is the author of *Colby's Book of the American Pit Bull Terrier.*

Heather Cosgrave resides in Georgia with her husband Matthew and their three Chinese Crested dogs. They devote their time and love to homeless and needy animals as well. Please visit *www.thedancingdog.com* to learn more.

Barbara Croke was born and raised in Brooklyn, where she lives with her dog Bullet.

Kerry Dahlheim has been doing Jack Russell terrier rescue in Omaha, Nebraska, for seven years. Kerry has successfully rehomed more than 100 dogs.

Sandi Davis is thirty-five years old and was born with spinal muscular atrophy. Sandi has been in a wheelchair since she was five. She has a bachelor's degree in speech therapy and masters' degree in special education.

Mike de la Flor is a medical illustrator, instructor, and published author, but more important, he is a husband, dad, and dog lover. He recently completed *The Carrara Studio 3 Handbook* and is starting a second book titled *Creating Biomedical Illustrations.*

Donna Echenrode lives in Arizona with her family of two dogs and one cat, her daughter with her two horses and three dogs, and her son with his two cats. To complete the family with their first grandchild expected, Donna's stepson and his wife have three dogs. Donna says of her life, "Animals abound!"

Audrey Elias lives in Brooklyn, New York, with her husband, three children, a two-year-old German shepherd named Nemo, and two cats (down from a personal best of nine).

Catherine Raven Feher-Elston is the author of *Wolfsong: A Natural and Fabulous History of Wolves*; *Ravensong: A Natural and Fabulous History of Ravens and Crows*; and *Children of Sacred Ground*. Her family includes wolves, ravens, Alaskan malamutes, and a foundling pup.

Mary Frenzel-Berra grew up in Ironton, Missouri, a small Ozarks town. She resides in Brooklyn, New York, with Bob Frenzel-Berra, Bazil's Dawn Treader, CDX, CGC, and Dalin's Pushkin, CD, CGC, Therapy Dog International.

Robert Frenzel-Berra is Director of Research and Program Development at the Department of Youth and Community Development in New York City.

Barbara Giella, Ph.D., is a former college professor who now has a dog training business in New York City named The Educated Puppy . . . and Dogs, Too.

Wendy Halling is a forty-six-year-old teacher in a small rural village school with sixty children enrolled.

Roni Henning is the author of the book *Screen Printing, Water-Based Techniques* (Watson-Guptill, Inc.).

Henry C. Hicks joined the Lexington Police in August of 1996. Officer Hicks's partner is a Belgian Malinois.

Pat Hill received her first guide dog in June 1977, a month after graduating from Boston College with her masters' degree in special education.

Lee Hough breeds working-line German shepherds under the kennel name Von Wolfstraum.

Neal C. Jennings founded Pets on Wheels of Scottsdale, Arizona, in 1990 and has directed the organization ever since.

Anthony Jerone is the owner and director of the Academy of K9 Education in Flushing, Queens.

Tracie Karsiens is twenty-seven years old and married. She works in the computer industry.

Peter Landy and his wife, Marysel, have a beautiful infant son named Robert and a handsome young German shepherd named Axel.

Fred Lanting is an internationally known behaviorist and consultant in orthopedics, training, structure, and everything else about the German shepherd. He has published numerous books and articles on the breed, including *The Total German Shepherd Dog* (Hoflin Pub., Ltd.). Fred has judged in dog shows throughout the United States and across the world.

Michael Leonard trains probation officers in criminal justice arrest and safety procedures, effective report writing, conflict resolution, defensive tactics, and handcuffing.

Dr. Sue Ann Lesser, D.V.M., practices in five states as a 100-percent chiropractic veterinarian.

Louise Maguire's childhood dream was to have a faithful canine friend like the beautiful collie in *Lassie Come Home* or *Lad of Sunnybank*.

Edy Makariw lives in a big city in a small house with her partner, two big, big dogs, and a few cats.

Michael Marino and his wife Josephine live in Staten Island, New York.

Julie Marlow owns and operates Vom Banach K9 in Port Orchard, Washington, besides her full-time job as mom for two growing sons and her work as an experienced veterinary technician for many years.

Anne Martindale lives with Trevor, an Airedale terrier, in rural upstate New York.

Elli Matlin, owner of Highland Hills German Shepherds, is a well-known third-generation dog breeder in Rock Hill, New York.

Gabrielle McGhee resides with her family in a beautiful rural area of upstate New York.

Bev McQuain owns and runs Llewellyn Security, now Canada's largest canine security company, where patrol, drug, and bomb dogs pay their own way so Bev can keep them all.

Jenny Moir lives in England where she heads up the public relations department for her agency, Hearing Dogs for Deaf People. Besides loving dogs as pets, Jenny's deep appreciation for them as service givers to people in need has made her particularly sensitive to the special talents of canine friends.

Bridgette Mongeon is a sculptor and writer residing in Houston, Texas, with her husband, two dogs, and two cats.

Ali Moore, an active mother of four, is the founder and director of Bulldawg Rescue of Georgia, Inc., a nonprofit organization dedicated to the rescue, rehabilitation, and rehoming of unwanted English bulldogs.

Stephanie Nolasco is a young student and writer residing in New York City.

Lonnie Olson is a dog trainer and founder of Dog Scouts of America, an organization founded to educate people about responsible dog ownership and the importance of the human/canine bond.

Bob Osgoodby lives in Sea Bright, New Jersey, with his wife Susan.

Deborah Palman has been training dogs since 1976, starting with hunting retriever training and trials and progressing to police K9, search-and-rescue, and Schutzhund training.

Heather Pate lives in British Columbia, Canada, with her husband, three harlequin Great Danes, and a Border collie mix.

Maxine Perchuk works in New York City as a probation officer assigned to family court.

Yvette Piantadosi-Ward has been breeding German shepherds and Malinois dogs for many years, as well as rescuing and rehoming lost dogs of every kind. She lives in Youngsville, North Carolina.

Donna Ramsay, a lifelong dog lover, currently lives in Phoenix.

Marcy Rauch was part of an early group of deaf dogs and owners that sought to educate many on the wonderful life these dogs could have, despite their deafness, and to show they were not the "disposable" dogs portrayed by many.

Mary Rodgers was born in Guanajuato, Mexico, and now makes her home in Grand Prairie, Texas.

Susan Rubin has been a professional photographer for over fifteen years working for many major magazines such as *Parade, Glamour, GQ, Self, Italian Vogue,* and *British Vogue.* She is currently working on a stylish book about dogs.

Jack Ryan is the public relations director of the New York City Department of Probation. He lives in Staten Island, New York, with his wife Diane, their four boys, three guinea pigs, and a golden retriever named Barney Ralph the Wonder Dog.

Marlene Sandler works as an animal communicator. She lives in Warrington, Pennsylvania.

Lori Sash-Gail has been a New York City dog trainer for fifteen years. Lori has been featured on the television show *Amazing Tails.* Her dog column was published in the *Nyack Villager,* and her photographs have been in *Bark Magazine,* the *ASPCA Animal Watch,* and *Delta Interactions.*

Claudette Schafer and her husband own and operate a small kennel in British Columbia, where they breed Alaskan malamutes.

Dottie Seuter lives in Great Neck, New York, with her husband, Evert. Her dogs have successfully competed in Schutzhund sport and AKC obedience, tracking, and agility trials.

Gail Smart was educated in the London suburbs where she grew up. After many varied job experiences, from farming with horses to working in a bank, Gail settled into IT for a multinational oil company until she retired to Kent where she lives with her dogs and cats, many of which are rescues.

Irene Smith is Founder and Director of the Animal Rescue Network of East Harlem (ARNEH), an all-volunteer animal rescue organization.

Gary Stafford and his wife Terri live in Maine and share their home with six canines.

Terri J. Stafford lives in rural Maine, where six dogs of various breeds currently own her. Terri trains dogs in obedience and does therapy work.

Rosemary Steele's job prevents her from owning a dog, but she enjoys a very special canine friendship with her friends' dog Jet.

Sara Stopek lives with her husband Robert, a dog named Emmett, and several cats in Clinton Hill, Brooklyn.

Paul Sutton (her mum wanted a boy!), fifty-five years young, lives in Kent, England, with her sister, her horse, three cats, and her three adored Border collies, Whisper, Summer, and Sunny.

Danielle Wiley is a Web content developer and freelance food writer living in Toledo, Ohio, with her husband, daughter, and a Weimaraner.

Permissions

Pages i, 193: Wilhelmenia O'Wunderbar Wuffenhofer. Maxine Perchuk, owner; Theresa Mancuso, photographer.

Page ix: Asko. Joe Moldovan, owner; Theresa Mancuso, photographer.

Page x: Casper. Irene Smith, owner; Theresa Mancuso, photographer.

Page 2 and 154: Beatrice Applebee. Maxine Perchuk, owner; Theresa Mancuso, photographer.

Page 24: Geisty and Abby. Theresa Mancuso, owner and photographer.

Page 44: Wilhelmenia O'Wunderbar Wuffenhofer. Maxine Percuk, owner and photographer.

Page 67: Marmaduke Rodgers and Abby. Theresa Mancuso, owner and photographer.

Page 82: Grip von der Starken. Theresa Mancuso, owner and photographer.

Page 105: Raffy. Dr. Nancy Bekaert, owner; Theresa Mancuso, photographer.

Page 175: Thunder. Karen McLean, owner; Theresa Mancuso, photographer.

Page 212: Sheena. Cindy Tibbits, owner and photographer.